dare to

bead

some more

dare to
bead
some more

heather laithwaite

METZ PRESS

Author's acknowledgements

Once again I need to say thank you to the many people whose help and understanding made this book possible for me. It has been a very busy year and I hope I have covered the many requests I received for a second book with lots of variety. For those who believed in me and asked me to teach far and wide, thank you.

To Tanya, my right hand and friend, thank you for all your help and all you do for me, testing my patterns, the many hours of work for this book and your help with the teaching – I do appreciate it so much.

To my students, thank you for such encouragement and love, for your enthusiasm as we all grow together, and for the worked pieces in this book. A special thank you to Betty Sheban for stepping in and helping when I need you. I value your support.

To Nikki, my illustrator, thank you for the hard work and enthusiasm, and putting your soul into the illustrations as well.

To Ivan, my photographer, thank you again for your patience and all you put into this second book – what can I say?

To Wilsia, my publisher and now my friend, I feel very privileged to have worked with you on my first book and now again. Thank you for making it all possible. What an experience!

Thanks also to Angie who did the lovely layout.

To my daughter, Tina, who waited so patiently for her pieces and gives me space to explore new grounds and indulge myself with my beads, thanks for your encouragement and joy at my development.

Thanks also to Steve and my two grandchildren, Cali and Sebastian, who view my beads with great joy.

To Mark, my youngest son who makes me so much larger than I am, I love you and thank you for sharing your family, Katinka and Kayra.

To Kevin, my eldest son who helped me so much with the computer and tried to make it easier for me with such patience despite all the phone calls at all times, thank you. And for your three beautiful children, Ethan and the twins, Anna and Dylan, who keep me young.

To Graeme, my husband, thank you for holding my hand and letting me grow, for giving me the latitude and space I needed to get this book done, for helping me source and buy materials and putting together the introduction. I know you enjoy the research as I pull you more and more into my world of beads. And thank you for my lovely studio – it will make a big difference. Thank you, my love, for all the love and support.

Published by Metz Press
1 Cameronians Avenue
Welgemoed, 7530
South Africa

First published in 2007
Copyright © Metz Press 2007
Text copyright © Heather Laithwaite
Photographs copyright © Metz Press

Publisher and editor	Wilsia Metz
Design and lay-out	Angie Hausner
Photographer	Ivan Naudé
Production assistant	Rowina Keiller
Illustrator	Nicky Miles
Reproduction	Positive Image, Epping
Printing and binding	Printed and bound in Singapore by Star Standard
ISBN	978-1-919992-58-7

Contents

Introduction

"Love the little trade which you have learned, and be content with it." Marcus Aurelius

For centuries beads have had significant meaning and purpose in everyday life, and so it continues to this day. It never ceases to amaze me how popular beading is and how many people from all ages and walks of life are benefiting from the therapeutic effects of this wonderful craft. In my first book, *Dare to bead*, I took my readers on an exciting journey to develop their skills through different projects, each one a little more complex and challenging than the previous one. I covered techniques such as tassels, spiral ropes, brick stitch and peyote stitch, each with a good number of projects to gain a good level of proficiency.

With this, my second book, I would like to continue this exciting journey, which will challenge the reader to new levels of creativity and offer tremendous rewards of achievement.

Stringing beads

Stringing beads is the simplest form of beading, but there are many other options, as you will see as you work through this book. There is such a vast array of beads on the market, that one could become quite bedazzled. Japanese seed beads are very small, with a relatively big hole, the popular sizes ranging from a very small 15°, followed by 11°, 8° and 6°. They are used mostly for bead weaving as the colour palette is enormous and the colours blend well. As far as quality and consistency are concerned, Japanese beads are truly unrivalled. Czechoslovakian seed beads come mostly in sizes 12°, 10°, 9°, 8° and 6°, all of which are suitable for beading, depending on the thickness of your thread medium. Bugle beads, on the other hand, are measured by their length in millimetres.

These beads are made from the same fine tubes as seed beads, but they are more tubular in shape and are also available in a twisted form. As far as quality is concerned, the Japanese bugle is far superior to the Czech or Chinese bugles. Always insist on using quality beads for your projects as you could really ruin your hard work by using beads which have rough edges that cut through thread with disastrous effect. If you do decide to use Czech or Chinese bugle beads, use a seed bead on either side of the bugle as this will prevent the thread from fraying. I generally prefer glass beads for most of my

projects, but there seems to be a huge swing to crystal as it produces just the most spectacular work.

THREAD MEDIUMS

Bead stringing, as the name suggests, is simply the stringing of single beads onto a variety of different threads or mediums. We will explore the different options for stringing, which include thin wire (with different diameters), multi-stranded flexible wire (Beadalon), DandyLine bead cord, Nymo thread and Tiger Tail. It's important to choose the right stringing medium as it will certainly affect your finished article if you use the wrong medium, leading to unwanted stretching if heavier beads are used, for example.

In this book different projects use different thread mediums. Stella, for instance, is sewn with Nymo thread, a strong thread made especially for beading, which comes on a bobbin in a variety of colours. As far as the needle is concerned, one must use a special beading needle with a small eye and shaft of similar diameter to easily pass it through beads. The most common sizes are size 12, 11 and 10. A size 22 tapestry needle can also be used successfully. Another type of needle which is popular, is a size 10 ballpoint bead-embroidery needle which has no sharp point and does not split the thread.

For Helen I used 0.8-mm diameter silver wire, which worked well for the larger beads as well as the small chips and 4-mm fire crystals. When choosing your stringing medium, use the largest diameter wire possible that will comfortably pass through the smallest bead hole in your design. Another hint is to choose a wire with a proper breaking strength consistent with the weight and type of beads being used, as the diameter of the wire is not always a good indicator of the strength. Choose the grade of wire that will allow your design to look, feel and hang the way you want it to.

Project Julia I strung with soft flex wire (Tiger Tail), a nylon coated stainless steel wire consisting of multiple strands. There are many options on the market, but my favourite is Beadalon, which is available in 7, 19, & 49 strands. Each strand type comes in up to 6 different diameters with different breaking strains. The number of strands inside the nylon coating determines the flexibility of the wire. Beadalon 49 is the most flexible and most professional quality wire and consists of 49 smaller wires stranded together for optimum flexibility. The greater the number of strands, the greater the flexibility. On Julia I used 0.38mm wire as it is quite thin and accommodated a 3 mm round bead and an 11° seed bead amongst the larger 8 mm beads.

I then made a piece of chain out of jump rings to embellish the front and attach the beads.

The Claire necklace was strung on ready-made chain, which is freely available, offers a large selection of styles as well as added interest and drama if used discriminately. Short lengths of chain lend a sparkling touch, and hanging a chain tassel from your design would give it a signature look. With Claire the beads are attached with thread using 11° seed beads through to 6mm large beads. I used Nymo thread, which is worked back and forth through the pattern.

I made the Jackie bracelet with ready-made silver-plated chain (which can be purchased in various lengths), and head pins, which come in a variety of lengths and can be cut to size. On this project I used beads ranging in size from 6 mm to 6°.

The excitement in this creative way of beading lies in experimenting with different mediums and beads and to dare to be different.

Stella lariat

Stella is a very simple single-strand necklace (lariat) made with needle and thread, using many different types of beads. You can use almost anything, but for this project I have chosen different bugles (the long cylindrical beads) of different sizes, then seed beads in three different sizes, and the round beads in two sizes. Use a very long thread, as it is all done in one piece, and pull the thread through the beads gently. There are many different ways of using this necklace. Wrap around the neck once, and tie in the front, or wrap twice around the neck. Another way is to fold the string in half and pull one side through the large 8-mm beads to stop the necklace from slipping (see page 21). The string can even be worn with jeans as a decoration.

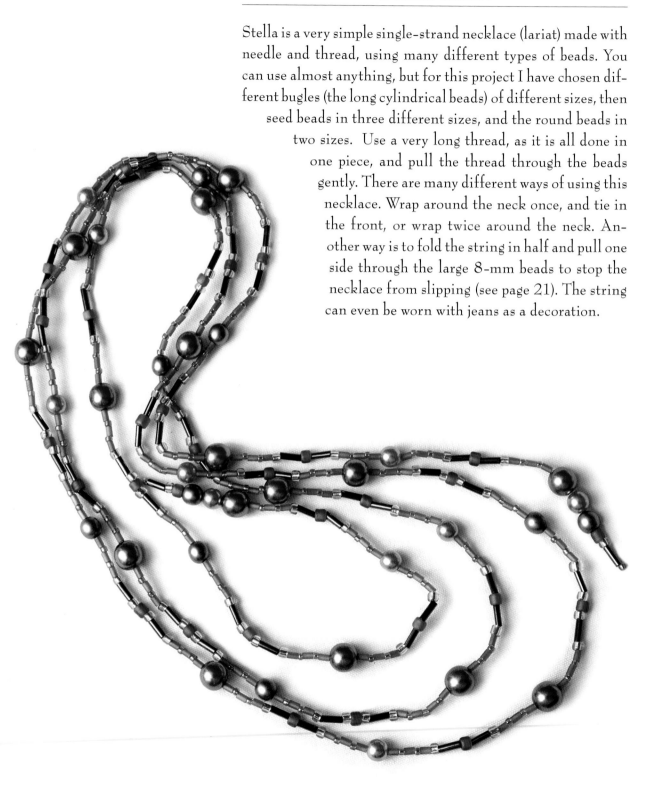

You will need
195A 3-mm bugles
75B 7-mm bugles
125C 11° seed beads, matching small bugles
105D 8° seed beads
45E 6° seed beads tonal to B
12F 6-mm round beads tonal to A
12G 6-mm round beads tonal to A
18H 8-mm round beads tonal to B
5 m strong nylon or Nymo-B thread
11 beading needle

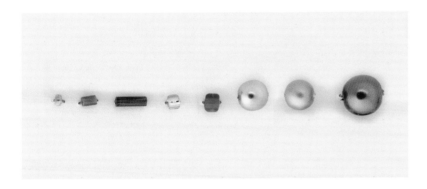

You start in the middle, so measure up 4 m of thread, winding 2 m around a piece of card with a slit will act as a bead stop and keep the thread tidy).

1. Pick up 1F (round 6-mm – the centre bead), * then 1A, 1C, 1A, 1C, 1A, 1D, 1B, 1D, 1E, 1D, 1B, 1D, 1A, 1C, 1A, 1C, 1A, 1H (round 8-mm).

2. 1A, 1C, 1A, 1C, 1A, 1D, 1B, 1E, 1B, 1D, 1A, 1C, 1A, 1C, 1A, 1G (round 6-mm).

3. Repeat step 1 from *.

4. Repeat step 2 but ending with 1F (round 6-mm).

5. Repeat step 1 from *.

6. Repeat step 2.

7. Repeat step 1 from*.

8. Repeat step 2 but ending with 1F (round 6-mm).

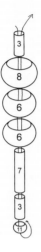

Fig A

Fig B

Reef knot

Right over left and under

Left over right and under

Left over right and under

Right over left and under

9. Repeat step 1 from*

10. Repeat step 2.

11. Repeat step 1 from*.

12. Repeat step 2 but ending with 1F (round 6-mm).

13. Repeat step 1 from*.

14. Repeat step 2.

15. Repeat step 1 from*.

16. Lastly pick up 1F, 1G, 1E, 1D, 1B, 1A, 1C, turn over the C and work back up to the start (Fig A).

17. Leave the thread here and unthread the needle. Thread up with the thread that was left in the middle on the card and work the second half from step 1 * (Fig B).

18. You will have two threads in the middle; tie them together, with a reef knot, (left over right and under, right over left and under). Work one thread down one half, knot and end with a dab of glue, then work the other thread down the other half in the same way.

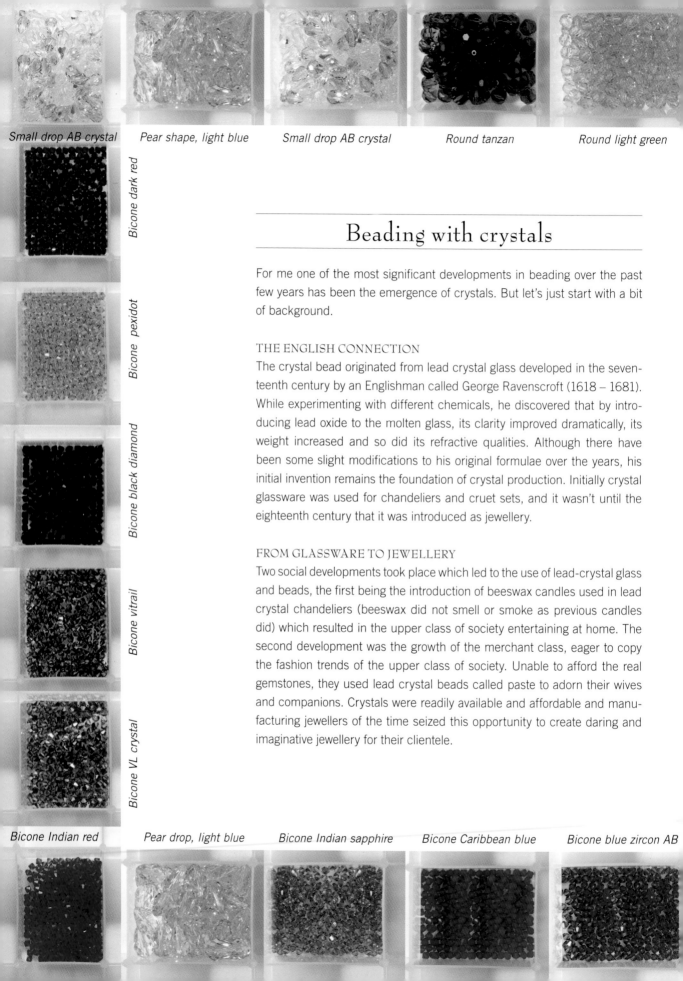

Small drop AB crystal   *Pear shape, light blue*   *Small drop AB crystal*   *Round tanzan*   *Round light green*

Bicone dark red

Bicone pexidot

Bicone black diamond

Bicone vitrail

Bicone VL crystal

Beading with crystals

For me one of the most significant developments in beading over the past few years has been the emergence of crystals. But let's just start with a bit of background.

THE ENGLISH CONNECTION

The crystal bead originated from lead crystal glass developed in the seventeenth century by an Englishman called George Ravenscroft (1618 – 1681). While experimenting with different chemicals, he discovered that by introducing lead oxide to the molten glass, its clarity improved dramatically, its weight increased and so did its refractive qualities. Although there have been some slight modifications to his original formulae over the years, his initial invention remains the foundation of crystal production. Initially crystal glassware was used for chandeliers and cruet sets, and it wasn't until the eighteenth century that it was introduced as jewellery.

FROM GLASSWARE TO JEWELLERY

Two social developments took place which led to the use of lead-crystal glass and beads, the first being the introduction of beeswax candles used in lead crystal chandeliers (beeswax did not smell or smoke as previous candles did) which resulted in the upper class of society entertaining at home. The second development was the growth of the merchant class, eager to copy the fashion trends of the upper class of society. Unable to afford the real gemstones, they used lead crystal beads called paste to adorn their wives and companions. Crystals were readily available and affordable and manufacturing jewellers of the time seized this opportunity to create daring and imaginative jewellery for their clientele.

Bicone Indian red   *Pear drop, light blue*   *Bicone Indian sapphire*   *Bicone Caribbean blue*   *Bicone blue zircon AB*

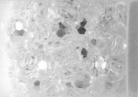
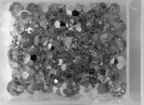

Round saphire *Round honey* *Round AB crystal* *Round VL crystal* *Round amethyst*

SWAROVSKI CRYSTALS

The next significant development was the introduction of the Swarovski crystal. To this day their beads are the ultimate standard in the world as far as quality, brilliance and colour perspective are concerned. Daniel Swarovski was born in Bohemia in 1862. His father had a small crystal cutting factory, and from an early age he watched and worked in his father's business. After completing his education in Paris, he spent time working and gaining experience with other crystal cutters before returning to his father's business. At the tender age of 21 he visited the "Erste Elektrische Ausstellung" (First Electrical Exhibition) in Vienna where he realized that he could harness the new lighting and electricity developed by Siemens and Edison to develop an automated cutting machine for crystals. After labouring night and day for nine years, he manufactured and registered a patent on a machine which cut crystals faster, more precisely and more accurately than could be done by hand at the time. In 1895 he moved to Wattens in the Austrian Alps, where there was enough water to power the machines and where he could protect the secrets of his new crystal-cutting and manufacturing process. This heralded a new era for Daniel Swarovski. He was soon joined by his brothers-in-law, Franz Weiss and Armand Kosmann, and the Swarovski empire was born.

Although Swarovski are the leaders in crystals, there are others with an equally fine reputation, Preciosa of the Czech Republic being one such house. You will find that once you have embarked on making items with crystals, life takes on a new dimension as far as the fine art of jewellery-making is concerned.

The crystals used for the projects in this book are among those captioned and illustrated on this page.

Bicone sapphire

Bicone amethyst

Round light blue

Round honey

Fire crystal teal

Bicone fire opal *Fire crystal gold* *Fire polish, light yellow* *Fire crystal red* *Fire crystal rose pink*

Working with wire

When working with wire, you need special tools and equipment not normally required for off-loom weaving.

PLIERS

As with everything else, using the right tool for a particular task makes it so much easier to achieve a professional finish. You will need several pairs of pliers for wirework.

Long-nose pliers – look for one that has a long nose and is fairly thin on the end, as this will give you more flexibility with the size of the rings you can turn. Also get a pair of chain-nose pliers and some round-nose pliers. Flat-nose pliers will be useful to hold the wire. You also need wire cutters. Make sure they are sharp so that you can cut the wire close to your work. Crimping pliers are used to squash crimps.

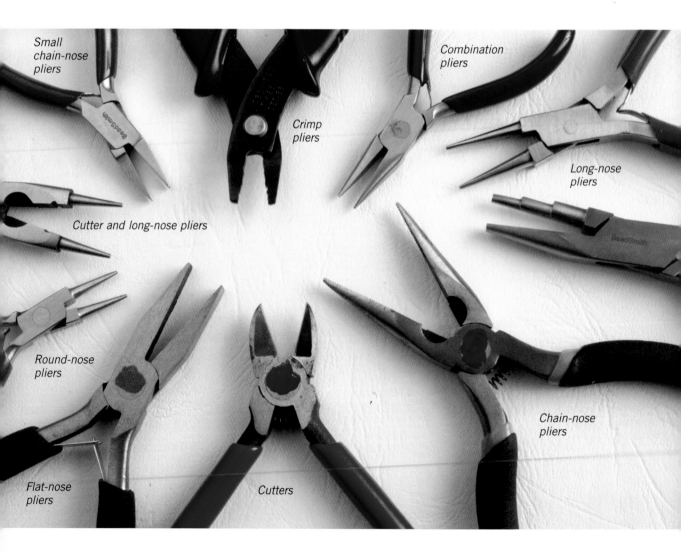

Small chain-nose pliers

Combination pliers

Crimp pliers

Long-nose pliers

Cutter and long-nose pliers

Round-nose pliers

Chain-nose pliers

Flat-nose pliers

Cutters

WIRE

Use good quality silver wire as you are putting a lot of effort into your bead-work and do not want to spoil the result by using sub-standard wire that will discolour and detract from the quality of the beads and craftsmanship. Silver-plated wire is inexpensive and readily available, while 925/sterling wire is expensive and fairly hard to come by.

Wire should be suitable for the beads you use – thicker wire for thicker beads, for example.

For Julia I used soft flex wire (Tiger Tail) in size 0.38. It consists of several different strands which are twisted together and then coated with nylon. It is much stronger than thread and ideal for stringing beads. It does not have the flexibility of thread, though, and you must be careful not to kink the wire, although today's versions are much more manageable.

EAR HOOKS AND STUDS

Use good quality – sterling silver or gold.

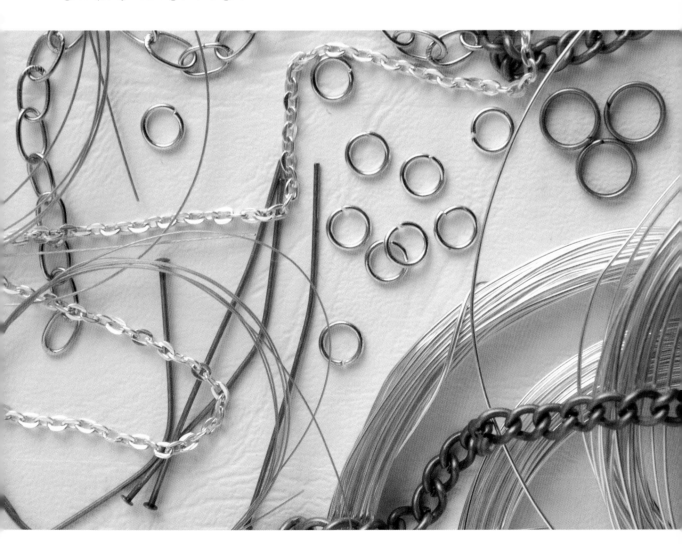

CRIMPS

If you want spaces between the beads, you could use crimps – little balls or tubes made of silver or other metals. Once they are threaded onto the wire, they are squashed with a pair of crimping pliers. They grip the wire, and stop the beads from sliding. Crimps are also used at the ends, near the clasp, as a way of fastening off. Using crimps with spaces between the beads is a quick way of threading some beads together for a special dance or birthday party.

HEAD PINS

A head pin is a piece of silver (or other metal) wire that looks like a normal pin but is elongated. They come in different lengths. I like to buy them a little on the long side, as there is nothing worse than struggling because it is too short when you have put on a couple of big beads. Buy 50 mm or longer. I like the 63 mm headpins.

First bead

Fig A

Fig B

Fig C

Fig D

Second bead

Fig E

Fig F

Fig G

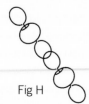

Fig H

Wire-chain loops

Wire-chain loops are used to attach bigger beads to one another. They are easy to make with the right tools.

First bead

1. Cut a 20-cm length of wire (any longer just gets in the way and there will be very little wastage from 20 cm) and thread up one of the long beads, with about 1 cm out the other side.

2. Use the flat-nose or chain-nose pliers and bend a right angle away from you at the point where the wire comes out of the bead (Fig A).

3. Use the round-nose pliers, grab the end of the wire at the very end and roll towards you, making a hanger (Fig B). The nearer to the front the pliers the smaller the loop. At this point I like to check that everything is straight, and if not, I just straighten it with my flat-nose pliers, then take the tip of the wire in the long-nose pliers and curl the hanger a little bit more.

4. Make sure you close it properly, or the next link will slip out (Fig C).

5. Now hold the little loop you have just made underneath close to the bead, cut the wire about 1 cm above the bead on the other side and make the next loop on this side (Fig D). Your first bead is done.

Cutting the wire

Bend a right angle

Grab the end of the wire

Roll towards you

Second bead

1. Leaving the wire on the length, bend a right angle about 1 cm from the end away from you, using your flat-nose or chain-nose pliers (Fig E).

2. Grab the wire at the end with the long-nose pliers and roll towards you making a hanger. Make sure that everything is straight, using the flat-nose pliers, then insert the hook into the loop from the first bead (Fig F).

3. Grip the wire at the end with the long-nose pliers and roll towards you for the rest of the way, making sure you close the loop properly (Fig G).

4. Place the next bead on the wire and cut 1cm away, making sure the last loop is sitting close onto the bead.

Last bead

Having made the connecting loop and placed the bead on, cut the wire 1 cm away, turn the hanger, and place it into the first bead to close the circle, and close the loop (Fig H).

Make a hanger

Cut the wire to make the next loop

Close the loop properly

Last loop close to the bead

Second bead hanger on to first bead

Second bead hanger on to first bead

Fig A

Fig B

Fig C

Fig D

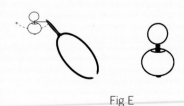

Fig E

Wrapped-chain loop

A wrapped-chain loop is a loop made with wire wrapped around the stem – a very safe way of hanging beads from a chain, as the wrapping ensures that the beads do not fall off at the connection point.

1. Place a head pin in your bead (Fig A). Grip the wire just above the bead with the chain-nose pliers and use the long-nose pliers to bend it at a right angle over the chain-nose pliers away from you (Fig B). You should have a bead with a stalk of about 2 mm, and then a right-angle bend.

2. Use the tip of the long-nose pliers to grip the wire at the bend (the nearer the front of the pliers you grip the smaller the loop), and use the chain-nose pliers to pull the wire over the top of the long-nose pliers towards you, making a hanger (Fig C).

3. Grip the top of the hanger with the long-nose pliers (I am right handed, and I find I hold the grip with my left hand, with the hanger towards the left, and the tip of the pliers towards me.) Use the other pliers to bend the wire around in front of you across the hanger. Cut the wire to about 50 – 60 mm.

4. Grip the loop across both sides with the chain-nose pliers and use the other pliers to wrap the extended wire down towards the bead, filling the gap between

Thread head pin through drop

Cross the wire

Make a small bend-kink

Wrap wire around straightened end

the first wrap and the bead. Make three to four wraps, cut the wire close to the bead and make sure there are no rough ends.

Wrapped loop from a drop

This technique is used in the Jackie bracelet (page 40) and the Theresa earrings (page 46).

1. Start at the bottom, with the drop. Cut off the head of a head pin and thread the head pin through the drop, almost half way (Fig A). Cross the wire over the top of the drop (Fig B).

2. Take one end of the wire and make a small bend-kink to straighten it upright (Fig C).

3. Grip the loop on both sides with the chain-nose pliers, wrap the wire around the straightened end using the other pliers and cut (Figs D and E).

4. Now make the loop, as in the wire-chain loop (see page 22) (Figs F and G).

5. Take another headpin, cut off the head, and make a wire chain loop (see page 22) (Fig G). Attach the loop from a drop, thread on a bead and make a wrapped loop (Fig H).

Fig A

Fig B

Fig C

Fig D

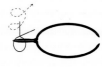
Fig E

Fig F

Fig G

Fig H

Make three to four wraps

Cut the wire

Thread on another bead

with wire 25

Helen necklace

This necklace is strung on wire, linked together to form a chain. Use good quality silver wire for the best results. I used a number of different beads. I like to use glass beads as they are heavier, hang better and look attractive — and there is such a lovely variety of beads to choose from. Start with the large bead and then collect around it. I used two colours in different tones and added chips as I enjoy them. Buy twice the recommended quantity as some of the holes are very small and will not allow the wire to pass through. Just put them away to use for another project with thinner wire or needle and thread. If your large focal beads have large holes buy more 4-mm beads to match the A focal beads, as they will sit on either side of each focal bead. Before you start, play with your beads and see how you would like them to lie, or follow the sequence I have made up.

You will need

5A large focal bead (about 40 x 12 mm)
15B facetted crystal rounds (10 mm)
40C large crystal chips (to match B)
5D oval beads (8 x 10 mm) (to match A)
5E round 10-mm beads (to match B)
5F round 8-mm beads (to match A)
10H facetted 4-mm beads (to match G)
5J facetted 4-mm beads (to match A) (10 moreif the A beads
have large holes)
5G large beads (150 x 14 mm)
2 m silver wire (0,8 mm)
Long-nose pliers
Flat-nose pliers
Round-nose pliers

Fig A

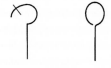

Fig B

Fig Bi

1. Cut a length of about 20 cm wire and bend a right angle about 1cm from the end away from you with the flat-nose pliers (Fig A).

2. Place the round-nose pliers at the end of the bent wire and roll towards you, making a hanger, then move the pliers into the curve and close the loop towards you. Do this at one end only (Fig B). Pick up 1A and place it on the wire. If the hole is large, pick up 1J first, then 1A and another 1J (FigBi).

3. Cut the wire 1cm away from the bead and, pushing the loop close to the bead, now take the flat nose pliers and bend the wire away from you and continue as in step 2. You will have a bead with a loop (and a little bead if the hole is large) on either side (Fig C).

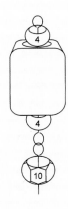

Fig C

4. Now working with what is left of the 20-cm length of wire, bend another right angle 1 cm from the end with the flat nose pliers as in step 1, then take the round-nose pliers and roll the wire towards you to make the hook, take the hook through the ring on the end of the focal A bead, and close the hook into a neat

round. Pick up the B bead, and place it onto the wire. Cut the wire 1cm from the bead and bend it away from you making a right angle, using the flat-nose pliers. Use the round-nose pliers to make another hook or hanger, and close it neatly.

5. Take a new piece of wire, bend, turn, and put the hook into the B bead loop, then close the loop. Pick up 1C, 1D and 1C, bend the right angle, then the hook, and close.

6. A new piece of wire, bend, hanger, connect, and close. Pick up 1E, cut, bend, hook, and close.

7. A new piece of wire, bend, hanger, connect and close. Pick up 1C, 1F, 1C, cut, bend, hook, and close.

8. A new piece of wire, bend, hanger, connect and close. Pick up 1B, cut, bend, hook, and close.

9. A new piece of wire, bend, hanger, connect, and close. Pick up 1H, 1G, 1H, cut, bend, hook, and close.

10. A new piece of wire, bend, hanger, connect, and close. Pick up 2C, 1J, 2C, cut, bend, hook, and close.

11. A new piece of wire, bend, hanger, connect, and close. Pick up 1B, cut, bend, hook, and close.

12. Repeat, steps 2-11 four more times, making this a nice long rope. The last B picked up when step 11 is repeated for the fourth time will then close into the first bead to close the circle.

Julia necklace

Try to use good beads for this multi-string piece, as they are more even and will achieve a good finish, making the time you spend on your project very worthwhile. I recommend using a two- or three-hole clasp when you start making multi-string pieces. You can use a single-hole clasp, but until you are familiar with the threading, using a double- or triple-hole clasp makes it easier to see which string is which. The piece is finished off with a tassel, just so that there is a focal point. This is made up with 6-mm jump rings forming a chain. When making a multi-string piece, I find it easier to work on a small bust prop. Others like to work on a beading tray with grooves. Whatever you prefer, have fun.

You will need

385B 11° seed bead
70C 3-mm round beads
58D 4-m round beads
18J 4-mm round beads
10L 4-mm round beads
20F 4-mm Bicone crystals
17A 6-mm round beads
13G 6-mm round beads
11K 6-mm round beads
17E 8-mm round beads
9M 8-mm round beads
9 stone chips
7 crimps
Double or triple clasp
(a clasp with two or three holes on either side)
9x6-mm jump rings
14x50-mm headpins
1,7 m 0.38 flexible beading wire
Chain-nose pliers
Long-nose pliers
Cutting pliers
Crimping pliers

Make small centre chain

Start by making a small chain through which each string passes. At the end, the tassel is also made onto this small chain.

Open a jump ring with the pliers as follows: holding one pair of pliers in each hand gripping the ring, pull one pair towards you and one pair away from you to prise a small opening. Slip two jump rings into it and close it, again with a pair of pliers in each hand, working them back and forth gently until you have closed the rings. (Never pull them sideways, as it will distort the ring). Now take the top ring, open it, place another jump ring in, and close. Repeat until you have 8 rings put together (Fig A, page 35).

Make the focal piece (Fig J)

1. Take a headpin and thread on 1K, 1B. Wrap the wire loop (see page 24) and attach to the first jump ring of the chain at the front.

2. Take another headpin and thread on 1E, 1B. Wrap the wire loop and attach to the second jump ring of the chain at the front.

3. Take another headpin and thread on 1M, 1B, wrap and attach to the third jump ring of the chain at the front.

4. Take another head pin and thread on 1D, 1L, 1C, 1B, and wrap. Attach to one side of the fourth jump ring. Take another headpin, thread on 1L, 1D, 1C, B, wrap and attach to the other side of the fourth jump ring.

5. Take the next headpin and thread on 1 chip, 1L, 1B, wrap and attach to one side of the fifth jump ring. Take another headpin and thread on 1G, 1D, 1B, wrap and attach to the other side of the fifth jump ring.

6. Take the next headpin and thread on 1A, 1J, 1B, wrap and attach to one side of the sixth jump ring. Take another headpin and thread on 1K, 1F, 1B, wrap and attach to the other side of the sixth jump ring.

7. Take the next headpin and thread on 1K, 1C, 1B, wrap and attach to one side of the seventh jump ring. Take another headpin and thread on 1G, 1J, 1B, wrap and attach to the other side of the seventh jump ring.

8. Take the next headpin and thread on 1M, 1F, 1B, wrap and attach to the eighth jump ring at the bottom. Take another headpin and thread on 1E, 1L, 1B and repeat.

Jackie bracelet

The Jackie bracelet is made up using the 0,6-mm silver wire in different ways, attached to a piece of chain, with links of about 5-6 mm. These are fun to make, and though I have set a pattern here, you can use beads at random, making this a good way of using up all those single beads you have left over from other projects. You can also make a necklace, using the beads on the front section, and just having the chain at the back. Have fun and create a different look with beads of all sizes.

You will need

2 jump rings

18-25 cm chain with links of 5-6 mm.

Toggle clasp

70-80 silver wire head-pins

33-45 x 6° seed beads in assorted colours

30-40 x 4-mm facetted fire crystals, matching colours of seed beads

25-32 x 4-mm squares, matching colours of seed beads

50-60 x 6-mm Gutermann round beads

9-14 x 8-mm round beads.

9-14 leaves or drops 11x5 mm

Chain-nose pliers

Long-nose pliers,

Cutters

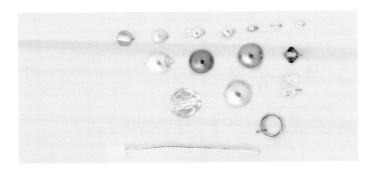

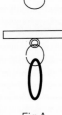

Fig A

Fig B

Fig C

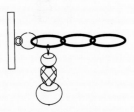

Fig C

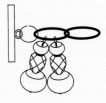

Fig D

Attach the clasp

Measure the chain around your wrist – it must connect with ease – and cut at that length. Mine is 18 cm long. Attach the clasp as follows. Take a pair of pliers in each hand and grip the jump ring on either side of the join. Pull one hand towards you and one hand away. (Never open jump rings by prising them apart, as they will distort.) Thread on the clasp as well as one end of the chain and close the jump ring in the same way, holding the pliers in each hand, working back and forth, until they close well (Fig A). Do the same on the other side of the chain.

First layer of embellishment

1. Thread onto a headpin a 6-mm round bead, a 4-mm fire crystal, and a 6° seed bead all of the same colour run (Fig B). Follow steps 1-4 for making a wrapped loop (see page 24) and slip the loop onto the first chain link before completing the wrapped loop (Fig C).

2. Using the second colour run, make another sequence of beads as above and slip into the same shared first link (Fig D).

Fig E

Fig F

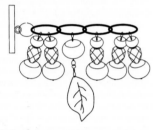

Fig G

Fig H

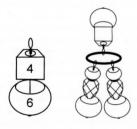

Fig I   Fig J

3. Using the third colour, make a wrapped loop from a drop (see page 25), starting with the drop or leaf, and then add a 6-mm round bead for the second piece. Attach the loop to the second chain link (Fig E).

4. Using the fourth colour, make another sequence of beads as in step 1 and attach into the third chain link (Fig F).

5. Using the fifth colour, make another sequence of beads as in step 1 and attach into the fourth chain link.

6. Using the sixth colour, make another sequence of beads as in step 1 and attach to the shared fourth chain link (Fig G).

7. Using the seventh colour, make another sequence of beads as in step 3 and attach to the fifth chain link (Fig H).

To complete the first layer, continue with the seven-colour run, and repeat steps 4, 5, 6 and 7 for position.

Second layer of embellishment

1. Thread onto a headpin a 6-mm round bead and a 4-mm square in the first colour (Fig I). Make a wrapped loop and attach to the first chain link, on the other side of the beads already sharing this link (Fig J).

2. Make another sequence of beads as above in the second colour and attach to the second chain link on the other side of the wrapped loop from a drop

3. Thread onto a headpin a 8-mm round bead followed by a 4-mm square in the third colour and attach it to the third chain link.

These steps form the pattern. Take it through the seven colours.

Jackie bracelet colour variation

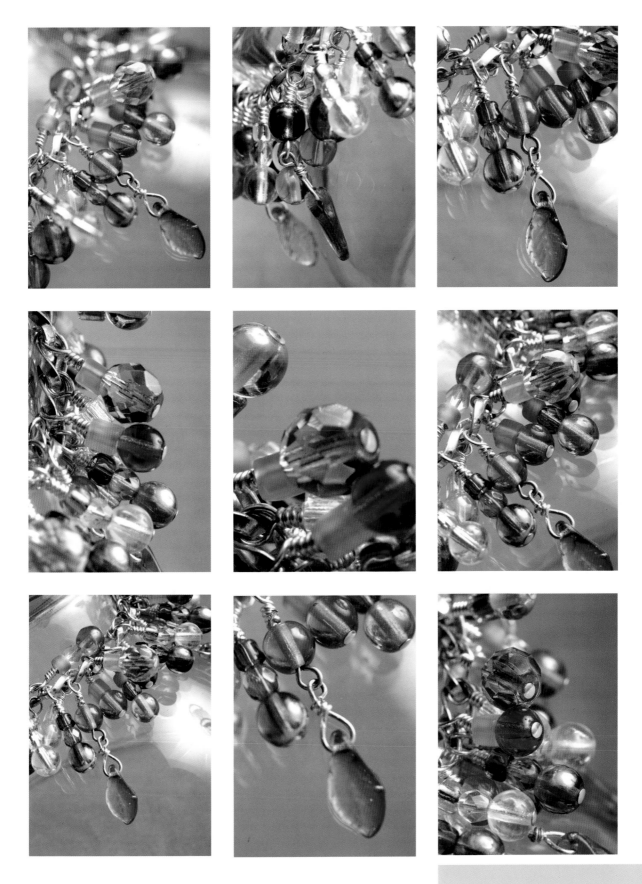

Theresa earrings

These little earring are good practice pieces to perfect the different ways of wrapping and working with chain. You can make them with any kind of bead, or dress them up by using crystal or pearls. They can be completed in a few minutes and make a lovely little gift for female guests at a dinner party. Or spoil yourself and make a new pair for each outfit to ensure you have earrings in just the right colour. You can make them on studs or hooks, whatever you prefer to wear. Only use studs and hooks of good quality. I prefer sterling silver or gold.

You will need
Two ear studs or hooks
4x 60 mm silver headpins
(these will be a little on the long side
but I prefer it that way)
2 large beads
(about 10 to 12 mm – not too big,
as this may be too heavy for the ear)
2 smaller beads (about 6 mm)
Chain-nose pliers
Round-nose pliers
Cutters

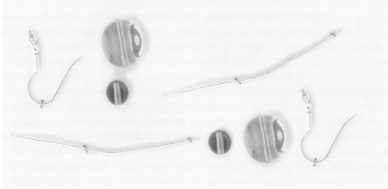

Fig K

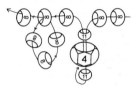

Fig L

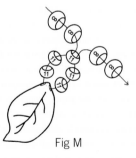

Fig M

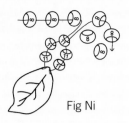

Fig Ni

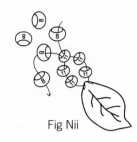

Fig Nii

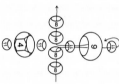

Fig O

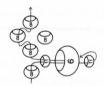

Fig P

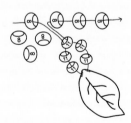

Fig Q

Fig R

2. Repeat until you have put on 17D leaves (Fig Ni), go through the top right angle bead, plus 1 more coming out at the side of the right angle. Pick up 3A, 1D, 2A, go back through the last A, and on around 1 more A in the right angle, then down 1B in the Y (Fig Nii).

3. Pick up a further 11D in the same way after each 2B, with the 11th the last one. Work down to the end and through the B and the A, and the D bead, turn back up the As and 20Bs coming out in the same space as the C (crystal) (Fig O).

4. Pick up 1A, 1E (6-mm), 1A, turn over the A, work back through the E and last A, then up the next 2B. Repeat until you have put on 6E beads (Fig P). You are about to go around the right angle.

5. Work up through 2B beads to the top of the right angle and back to the leaves. Pick up 3A, 1D, 2A and work back through the last A, up 2B again and up the second side (Fig Q).

6. Pick up 3A, 1D, 2A and work back through the last A, (making the loop) and then up the next 2B. Repeat until you have added a total of 17D leaves on the second side.

7. Travel up the last 7B beads, through the 6A beads (in the loop connecting the chain to the beads) and back down 15B to add 1E (6-mm) in the shared space with the crystal.

Part 3

1. Pick up 1A, 1E, 1A, needle and thread over the A and back through the E and the A, and down 2B heading towards the centre. Repeat until you have 13E beads, which will bring you out at the centre right angle. Go through 1 more B bead (the centre bead).

2. Pick up 1A, 1E, 1A, needle and thread over the last A, back through the E and the A. and up 2B up the other side. Repeat until you have added another 12E (13E beads in total).

Travel up to the end, knot again with the tail thread and travel up through the loop, back down, knot and end. Dab a little nail varnish on the last of the thread that you pull through to glue it. Do the same with the tail end and repeat with any joined thread.

To join a new thread, make an overhand knot (Fig R) with the two threads together and join close to where the thread is in the bead. Place a needle into the knot and guide down to the base.

Fig A

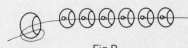

Fig B

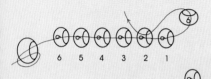

Fig C

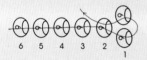

Fig D

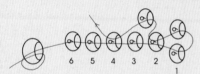

Fig E

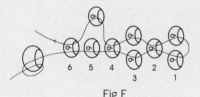

Fig F

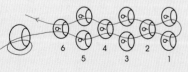

Fig G

Peyote stitch

Peyote stitch makes a softer fabric than brick stitch, thus its uses are endless. It is an off-loom stitch and the bead holes lie east and west (brick lies north and south). It makes a stronger fabric than brick because the thread passes through the beads more than once. Tension is thus also very important, because if it is too loose, the threads will show between the beads. Peyote can be done with one bead, which is the most widely used method. There is also two and even three drop peyote. All the beads are threaded onto a thread and grow from this point, therefore the foundation row is much easier to make than with brick stitch. As with brick stitch, however, it is vital that you use good quality beads to gain a nice, even fabric.

Even-count flat peyote

This is the easiest peyote stitch, but because there is no centre point, patterns are a bit of a challenge.

1 Thread a stop bead that is different from those with which you are working (Fig A). Thread any even amount of beads (for example 8, 10, 12), and push them down to the stop bead (Fig B).

2 Working from right to left, pick up a bead and take the needle over the last 2 beads nearest the needle and into the 3rd bead from the needle (Fig C). This will give you two beads lying side by side, both threads passing through the next bead – 2nd bead on the foundation row (Fig D).

3 Pick up another bead, miss the next (3rd) bead on the foundation row, and into the next (4th) bead in the foundation row. Continue in this fashion for the row. You will have 2 beads on the end where you began the second row, and then one bead with both threads running through. Then 2 beads again, back to one bead, and so on (Fig F, G).

4 Having completed the row, go back and snug up all the beads so that they sit like a ladder. You should always end the row with one bead on the base with both threads going through the bead next to your stop bead (Fig G).

5 Row three, turn. Because you always end up with a single bead on the previous row, you will always start the new row with a bead. Pick up a bead and needle into the first proud bead of the previous row – 2nd bead in (Fig J). Pick up a bead, miss a bead, and needle into the next proud bead. Continue … again finishing with both threads running through the end bead (Fig I, J).

This stitch can be worked back and forth, but I find that my tension changes a little, so I like to turn my work and work mostly from right to left.

New thread

If your thread is becoming too short, (French) knot into the thread next to the bead at the end of the row (if possible). Take a new thread and weave into the work as illustrated on the right. Coming out where you left off, continue with the new thread, and then go back after having worked a few rows. Re-thread the old thread and weave into the new work, knot and travel and cut. I never like to cut on a knot, because it just might come loose, so I always travel before cutting.

To end a thread

Just weave your thread back into the work, knot and cut as explained above.

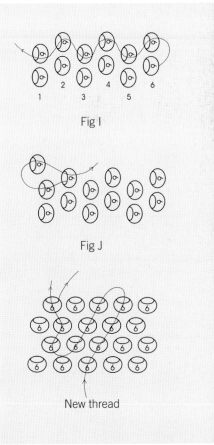

Fig I

Fig J

New thread

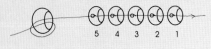

Fig A

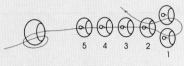

Fig B

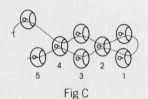

Fig C

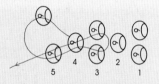

Fig D

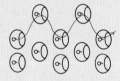

Fig E

Fig F

Fig G

Odd-count flat peyote

The technique for odd-count peyote is much the same, the only difference being in the turn at the end of the row. You start with an odd number of beads, thus pattern making is much easier because there is a central point from which to work. I like to think of odd-count peyote as being made up of long rows (adding the outside beads) and short rows (the outside beads are there already).

1 Thread a stop bead. Pick up any odd number of beads (for example 9, 11, 13) and push them down to the stop bead (Fig A).

2 Working from right to left, pick up a bead and take the needle over the last 2 beads nearest the needle and into the 3rd bead from the needle. This will give you 2 beads lying one above the other, with thread running through each of the beads (Fig B), and then both threads passing through the next bead – 2nd bead on the foundation row (Fig B), all the way to the end of the row. You will end up with both threads through a bead. Pick up a bead and take your needle from the top down through the last bead of the previous row (Fig C), and the next 2 (3 beads) – Fig D. The needle is taken across into the row you have just made and up the 3rd bead (Fig D) and across again to the first row and up to the top and out. Take your needle through the one bead standing proud. Continue your rows. The next row will be an inside or short row, as the outside bead is there already (Fig E).

3 INSIDE ROW Work a normal row (as in Fig E), your thread out of the outer bead. Pick up a bead and through the next proud bead, pick up another bead, and through the next proud bead, continue for the row (Fig F). The first and the last beads will always be on the inside of the outer bead (Fig G), hence it is called an inside row. The last bead will have both threads going through it.

4 OUTSIDE ROW In this row you will be putting in the end beads with the turnaround. One side is preformed as normal peyote (Fig H) – the start of the row. The other side has a turn – the end of the row. To start the row, pick up a bead (the end bead), and go through the next proud bead (Fig H). Continue to the end of the row, where you will pick up a bead (the end bead) and have nowhere to go (Fig I). So now take your needle from the top through the bead on the end of the previous row, and down through 3 beads, turn and back up to the top (Fig J). Take your needle back through the bead you have just put on, ready to start the inside row (Fig J).

The rows are made up with an inside row, then an outside row, continue.

Decrease on the outer edge

Complete the row and then make a turn as in odd-count peyote. Come out of the 2nd bead, or the first proud bead (see diagram on the right below). The decrease will happen on the ends of the rows.

Decrease in the middle of the row

Put your needle through 2 beads and pull up tight. These 2 beads will be counted as 1 in the next row.

Increase in the middle of the row

Pick up 2 beads together and go through the next bead, increasing the number of beads to the row. The next row, when you insert a bead for every bead in the row it will return to normal, just having the extra number of beads.

Flat circular peyote

Start with a few beads (3–5) and tie them into a circle using a reef knot (left over right, and right over left). Take your needle through the first bead.
The next row will be an increase (2 beads together for each bead in the row), so if you put on 3 beads in the beginning, the second row will have an increase for each bead, giving you 6 beads.

The next row will be a normal row of one bead in each space. The following row, try increasing in each space again. And so you will build your circle, with the number of increases depending on how big you want it.

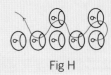

Fig H

Fig I

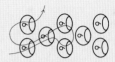

Fig J

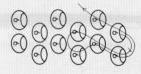

Decrease on outer edge

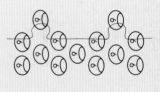

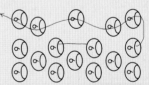

Decrease middle of row

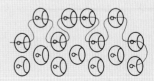

Increase middle of row

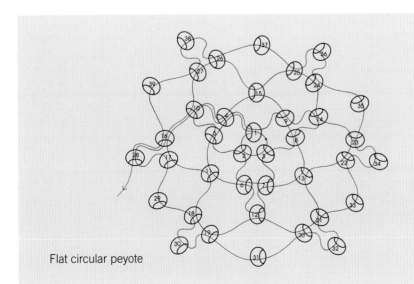

Flat circular peyote

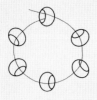

Fig A

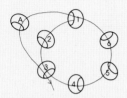

Fig B

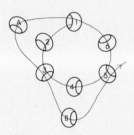

Fig C

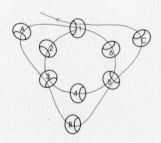

Fig D

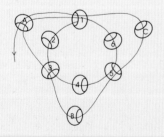

Fig E

Even-count tubular peyote

Even-count tubular peyote starts with an even number of beads (4, 6, 8, and so on), and after each row you make a step up. The advantage of this is that the top is kept very nice, even and flat, with a very neat finish.

1 Pick up 6 beads, make a circle by tying into a knot (left over right, and right over left). Working anti-clockwise, take the needle through the first bead to the left, as is better not to start on the knot (Fig A).

2 Pick up bead A, take it down the thread, then miss a bead on the circle from where your thread came out, and take the needle through the next bead – 3rd bead (Fig B).

3 Pick up bead B and take it down the thread, then miss the next bead on the circle from where your thread came out, and put your needle through the next bead – 5th bead (Fig C).

4 Pick up bead C and take it down the thread, miss the next bead from where your thread came out, and needle through the next bead – the 1st bead (Fig D). Then step up into the new row, taking the needle through bead A as well (Fig E).

Each row you will put in 3 beads. After the 3rd bead has been put in you will need to step up (the last bead in the row), and then step up into the new row you have just completed.

Odd-count tubular peyote

In odd-count tubular peyote you start the tube with an odd number of beads (5, 7, 9), which allows you to spiral up continuously. The only problem is that you will not have a flat top. There will always be one bead standing up on the top row, which is something you must consider when designing. It is the same technique as even-count, without the step up.

1 Pick up 7 beads and tie into a knot. Working anti-clockwise, take the needle through the first bead to the left. It is better not to start on the knot (Fig A, B).

2 Pick up a bead and take it down the thread. Now miss a bead on the circle from where your thread came out, and put your needle through the next bead – 3rd bead (Fig C).

3 Pick up another bead and take it down the thread. Miss a bead on the circle from where your thread come out, and put your needle through the next bead – 5th bead (Fig D).

4 Pick up a bead and take it down the thread. Miss a bead on the circle from where your thread came out, and put your needle through the next bead (7th bead on the circle). You have used all the beads on the circle, and will now be working on the spiralling (Fig E).

5 Pick up a bead, take it down the thread, and go through the 1st bead of the second row. At this stage you may find it a helpful to get a toothpick or a small knitting needle to insert it into the centre hole. Pull up the thread and you will now have 4 beads that stand up above the others. These are the 4 in which you will work. There will be 1 bead, a gap another bead, a gap, and 2 beads close together (Fig F).

6 Pick up another bead, miss a bead and go through the next, and so you go on, only going through the ones that stand proud. Always miss one bead and go through the next – the one standing proud (Fig G).

Try making the first part of the peyote project necklace on its own until you get the rhythm and understanding.

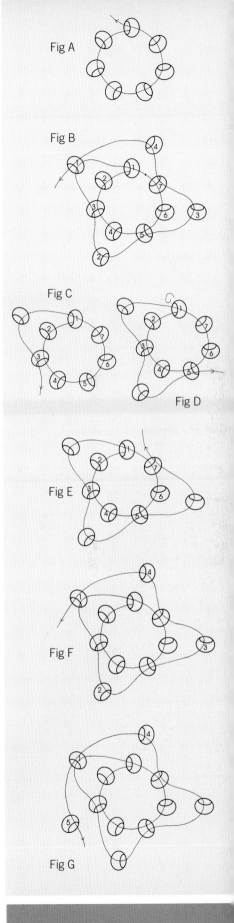

Fig A

Fig B

Fig C

Fig D

Fig E

Fig F

Fig G

Tammy scarf

Tammy is made up using peyote stitch with needle and thread. You will make a straight piece of peyote which you will join to make a tube. From the straight piece you will see that you can make a bracelet or chocker in the same way by adding a few more beads to the first row. If you do so, keep the number even. For this piece I used 60. You can try 80. Put a jump ring through an end bead and attach a clasp. The more even the beads the nicer the peyote stitch will look, so use good beads. I used Japanese beads as the holes are large in proportion to the size of the bead. You have to do a lot of ending off, back and forth in the beads from all the different strings. I used Nymo B thread – a nice strong thread that is not too thick. For the peyote piece, choose a colour that blends with the beads.

You will need

1400A 11° seed beads (main colour)
100C 11° seed beads (high-light)
1200G 11° seed beads (bright second string)
800J 11° seed beads (light third string)
800K 11° seed beads (medium fourth string)
400D 8° seed beads
60F 6° seed beads
70H 4-mm Gutermann round beads (pearl)
48x4-mm crystal bicones
12x8-mm fired crystals
25 m Nymo B thread
#11 beading needle

Make the tube

1. Thread the needle with about 2 m of thread and put on a stop bead, going through it twice with the back of the needle or without a needle (it is important not to split the thread, as the bead has to be removed later,) leaving a tail of about 20 cm at the end. Pick up 60A beads and take them down the thread, to the stop bead (Fig A).

2. Pick up 1A, miss the first A next to the needle, and needle into the second (Fig B). Pick up another A, miss an A and needle into the next. Continue through the row to the end, putting on 30 beads with the needle going through the last bead. You will end up with a ladder effect. Row 1 will become rows 1 and 2, hence row 2 will become row 3 (Fig C).

3. Pick up 1A and needle through the next proud bead (Fig D). Note that you will start each row picking up a bead. Continue until you have worked 16 rows. You will end with 8 beads on each straight side of your peyote piece to count the rows (Fig E).

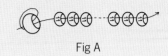

Fig A

Fig B

Fig C

Fig D

Fig E

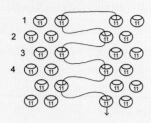

Fig F

Fig G

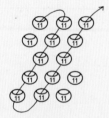

Fig H

Fig J

Make the tube, step 1

Make the tube, step 2

Make the tube, step 2

Closing the tube, step 4

Closing the tube, step 4

Ending off, step 5

4. Fold your work long sides together, and you will find your thread comes out of one short row, and on the other side is a long row – the two will fit together like a zip. Take your needle down the proud bead on row 1, go through the proud attached bead on row 2, go through the proud attached bead on row 3 and continue until you have gone through 60 beads, one side to the other (Fig F).

5. To end off, come out of the proud bead and up diagonally through five or more beads, then down the next row back to the top (Fig G), knot and weave your thread away.

Make the strings

You will make eight strings of slightly different lengths on each side. The dominant colour of each string is given in brackets to make it easier to follow where you are. For each string you add, cut a piece of thread 1,3 m and fasten it into the work as follows: enter up the end bead and travel down towards the middle of the worked piece through four to five beads diagonally, slip across to the adjacent bead and back through four to five beads to the end again (Fig H). Make a knot: take the needle through thread between the beads on the end, making a loop, and bring the needle through the loop from the back. Take the needle up the bead on the left and slip across to the bead on the right and out (Fig J). Cut off the tail.

1. Make the first string in A. Pick up (10A) 1G, 1C, 1G, (10A) 1G, 2D, (10A) 1G, 1D, 1H, 1D, (10A) 1G, 1D, a 4-mm crystal, (10A) 1G, 1C, 1G, (10A) 1G, 2D, (10A) 1G, 1D, 1H, 1D, (10A) 1G, 1D, 1F, (10A) 1G, 1C, 1G, (10A) 1G, 2D, (10A), 1G, 1D, 1H, 1D, (10A) 1G, 1D, 4-mm crystal, (10A) 1G, 1C, 1G (10A) 1G, 2D, (10A) 1G, 1D, 1H, 1D, (10A) 1G, 1D, 1F, (10A) 1G, 1C, 1G, (10A) 1G, 2D (10A) 1G 1D, 1H, 1D, (10A) 1G, 1D, a 4-mm crystal, 1D, an 8-mm fire crystal, 1A. Turn over the A and work back into the 8-mm fire crystal, 1D, 4-mm crystal and all the way to the top (Fig K) where the string meats the peyote.

2. End off by pulling the thread tight so that there is no slack, and work up the peyote tube in a diagonal line from the string by the number of beads in brackets (Fig L), make a circle stitch and work up a few more beads. Cut away the thread.

3. Make the same string on the other side of the tube, in the same position as the first one so that you will have 2 strings.

4. Make the second string in G. Thread up with 1,3 m, fasten into your work and pick up 3A, 1G, 2A, 2G, 1A, 9G, 1C, 1K, 1C, (18G) 1C, 2D, (18G) 1C, 1D, 1H, (18G) 1C, 1D, 4-mm crystal (18G) 1C, 1K, 1C, (18G) 1C, 2D, (18G) 1K, 1D, 1H, (18G) 1D 1F, 1D, (18G) 1C, 1K, 1C, (18G) 1C, 2D, (18G) 1D, 4-mm crystal, (18G), 1C, 1K, 1C, (18G) 1C, 2D, (18G) 1C, 1D, 1H, 1D, an 8-mm fire crystal,1G. Turn over the G and work back through the 8-mm fire crystal, D, H, D, B, and all the way to the top of the string and end off by repeating step 2.

5. Make the same string on the other side of the tube. If the second string is on the right of the first string, it should be on the left on the other side so that they fall more or less in the same place.

6. Make the third string in J. Thread up with 1,3 m, fasten into your work and pick up 3A, 1G, 2A, 2G, 1A, 1G, 1J, 1C, 1G, 1C, (11J) 1G, 2D, (11J) 1G, 1D, 1H, (11J) 1G, 1D, a 4-mm crystal, 1D, (11J), 1G, 1C, 1G, (11J), 1G, 2D, (11J), 1G, 1D, 1H, (11J), 1G, 1D, 1F, 1D, 1G, (11J), 1G, 1C, 1G, (11J), 1G, 2D, 1G, (11J), 1G 1D 1H, (11J), 1G, 1D, 4-mm crystal, 1D (11J), 1G, 1C, 1G, (11J), 1G, 2D, (11J), 1G 1D, 1H, (11J), 1G, 1D, 1F, 1D, (11J), 1G, 1D, a 4-mm crystal, 1D, (11J), 1G, 1C, 1G, (11J), 1G, 1D, a 4-mm crystal, an 8-mm fire crystal, 1G. Turn over the G and work back up the 8-mm crystal, D, G, (11J) all the way to the top of the string and end off by repeating step 2.

Fig K

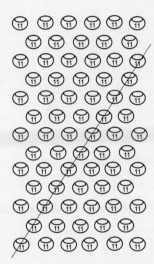

Fig L

7. Make another string on the other side next to the G string.

8. Make the fourth string in K. Thread up with 1,3 m, fasten into your work and pick up 3A, 1K, 2A, 2K, 1A, 6K, 1G, 1C, 1G, (15K), 1G, 2D, (15K), 1G, 1D, 1F,1D, (15K), 1G, 1D, 1H, (15K), 1G, 1D, a 4-mm crystal, (15K), 1C, 1G, 1C, (15K), 1G, 2D, (15K), 2D, 1H,1D, (15K), 1G, 1D, 1F, 1D, (15K), 1G, 1C, 1G, (15K), 1G, 2D, (15K), 1G, 1D, 1H, (15K), 1G, 1D, a 4-mm crystal, 1D, (15K), 1G, 1D, 1F, 1D, 1G, (15K), 1G, 1D, 1F, 1D, an 8-mm fire crystal, 1G. Turn over the G and work back up the 8-mm crystal and all the other beads all the way to the top of the string. End off by repeating step 2.

9. Make another string on the other side next to the J string.

10. Make the fifth string in J. Thread up with 1,3 m, fasten into your work and pick up 3A, 1G, 2A, 2G, 1A, 8J, 1G, 1A, 1G, (17J,) 1G, 2D, (17J), 1G, 1D, 1H, 1D, (17J), 1G, 1D, a 4-mm crystal, 1D, (17J), 1G, 1A, 1G, (17J),1G, 1D, 1H, 1D, 1G, (17J), 1G, 2D, 1G, (17J), 1G, 1D, 1F 1D, 1G, (17J), 1G, 1D, 1H, 1D, 1G, (17J), 1G, 1A, 1G, (17J), 1G, 2D, 1G, (17J), 1G, 1D, 1F, 1D, 1G, (17J), 1G, 1D, 1H, 2D, a 4-mm crystal, 1G. Turn over the G and work back up the 4-mm crystal and all the other beads all the way to the top of the string. End off by repeating step 2.

11. Make another string on the other side next to the K string.

12. Make the sixth string in G. Thread up with 1,3 m, fasten into your work and pick up 3A, 1G, 2A, 2G, 1A, 3G, 1H, 1A, 1K, (12G), 1K, 2D, (20G), 1K, 1D, 1H, 1D, (12G), 1K, 1D, a 4-mm crystal, 1D, 1K, (12G) 1K, 1A, 1K, (12G), 1K, 2D, 1K, (12G), 1K, 1D, 1H, 1D, 1K, (12G), 1K, 1D, 1F, 1D, 1K, (12G), 1K, 1D, 1K, (12G), 1K, 2D, (12G), 1K, 1D, 1H, 1D, 1K, (12G), 1K, 1D, a 4-mm crystal, 1D, 1K, (12G), 1K, 2D, 1H, (12G) 1K, 1D, 1F, 1D, 1K, (12G), 1K, 1D, 1H, 1D, 1K, (12G), 1K, 2D, 1K, (12G), 1K, 2D, 1H, a 4-mm crystal, 1G. Turn over the G and work back up the crystal, H, 2D, 1K, all the way to the top of the string. End off by repeating step 2.

13. Make another string on the other side next to the J string.

14. Make the seventh string in A. Thread up with 1,3 m, fasten into your work and pick up 16A, 1K, 1J, 1K, (16A), 1J, 1K, 2D, 1J, (16K), 1J, 1K, 1D, 1F, 1D, 1K, 1J, (16A), 1J, 1K, 1D, 1H, 1D, 1K, 1J, (16A), 1J, 1K, 1D, a 4-mm crystal, 1D, 1K, 1J, (16A), 1J, 1K, 1J, (16A), 1J, 1K, 2D, 1K, 1J, (16A), 1J, 1K, 1D, 1F, 1D, 1K, 1J, (16A), 1J, 1K, 1D, 1H, 1D, 1K, 1J, (16A), 1J, 1K, 1D, a 4-mm crystal, 1D, 1K, 1J, (16A), 1J, 1K, 1D, 1H, 1D, 1K, 1J, (16A), 1J, 1K, 1H, a 4-mm crystal, 1G. Turn over the G and work back up the crystal, the H, K, J, and all the way to the top of the string. End off by repeating step 2.

15. Make another string on the other side next to the G string.

16. Make the eighth string in K. Thread up with 1,3 m, fasten into your work and pick up 3A, 1K, 2A, 2K, 1A, 4K, 1A, 1J, 1A, (13K), 1A, 2D, (13K), 1J, 1D, 1H, 1D, 1J, (13K), 1J, 1D, a 4-mm crystal, 1D, 1J, (13K), 1A, 2D, 1A, (13K), 1J, 1D, 1H, 1D, 1J, (13K), 1A, 1J, 1D, 1F, 1D, 1J, 1A, (13K), 1J, 1D, a 4-mm crystal, 1D, 1J, (13K), 1J, 1D, 1H, 1D, 1J, (13K), 1A, 2D, 1A, (13K), 1A, 1J, 1A, (13K), 1J 1D, 1H, 1D, 1J, (13K), 1A, 1J, 1D, 1F, 1D, 1J, 1A, (13K), 1J, 1D, a 4-mm crystal, 1D, 1J, (13K), 1J, 1D, 1H, 1D, 1J, (13K), a 4-mm crystal, an 8-mm crystal, and 1A. Turn over the A and work back up the crystals, 13 K and all the way to the top of the string. End off by repeating step 2.

17. Make another string (the last) next to the A string on the other side. Work away any threads that may have been left, and dab a little nail varnish on the ends of the threads before pulling them through for the last time.

Cindy necklace and lariat

For this project you will use even-count tubular peyote which is a little more tricky than flat peyote, as you have to step up at the end of a row (see page 58), the advantage of which is a neat edge at the top. You can see this in the flower. In this project you will also increase in the middle of a row (when you make the flower). The necklace is made in two pieces knotted together to give length. This is the lariat part. But it can also be worn as a round necklace, with a small focal piece at the front, and worn much shorter. I used Gutermann beads in size 9°, a little bigger than the 11° but not big enough to look chunky, yet allowing you to grow the necklace a little quicker than if you had used 11° seed beads.

You will need
80F 14° seed beads (same colour as A)
800A 9° seed beads (tube and flower)
600B 9° seed beads (tube)
600C 9° seed beads (tube and stamen)
7D baby drops (flower)
3 large beads (1 round 6-mm, 1 round 8-mm and 1 shaped bigger bead)
Clasp
6 m Nymo B thread
#11 beading needle

Make the rope

1. Thread up with a nice long thread of about 2,5 m and pick up 1A, 1B, 1A, 1B, 1A, 1B, (6 beads). Take the beads down your thread leaving a tail of about 30 cm, tie a knot (reef knot, see page 20) and take the needle through your B bead. working to the left (Fig A).

2. Pick up 1C, miss the A bead and needle through the B bead (Fig B). Pick up another C, miss the next A and through the next B bead. Pick up your last C, miss an A bead and through the last B (this is the B you first took your needle through). Snug up – you should have 3 C beads sitting on the top. These are the beads you will work through next (Fig C). Now you will step up into the row above, through the C bead (this is the first C bead you put on.

3. Pick up 1A, needle through the C, bead (three times) and then step up into your first A bead. (you should have 3A beads on the top standing up).

4. Pick up 1B, needle through the A bead (three times) and then step up into your first B bead (you should have 3B beads on the top, standing up).

5. Pick up 1C, needle through the B bead (three times) and then step up into your first C bead (you should have 3C beads on the top, standing up).

6. Repeat steps 3 to 5 until your rope measures 50cm.

7. To end, go through the last 3 beads twice, to pull up and close the opening. Pick up 4F, half of your clasp, another 4F and work through the 3 end beads from the other side, making a shank. Repeat until you have 3 threads running through your 4F clasp, 4F, for strength. Fasten off. and repeat with the other half of the clasp (see Fig O, page 79).

Make the tassel

1. Pick up 3A, 3B, 3A, 3B, 3A, leaving a tail of about 30 cm. Place these beads around the rope, and go through all the beads again from the tail side up, making a ring over the rope, and tie a reef knot (Fig D).

2. Now Pick up 3B, 3A, 3B, 3A, 3B, plus the large shaped bead and 1A. Turn over the little A bead, needle back up the large bead, and all the way up the stem, and knot to the tail (Fig E).

3. Now work down the 3B and 3A, pick up 3A, 3C, the 6-mm round bead and 1C. Turn over the C bead and back up the 6-mml round bead, 3C and 3A, and back up 3A in the stem (Fig F).

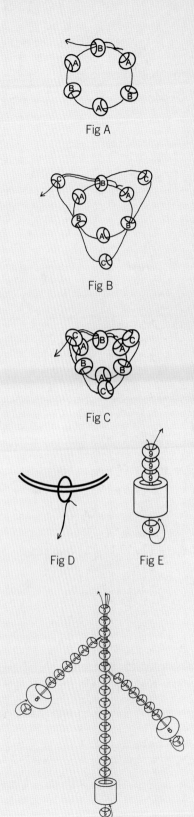

Fig A

Fig B

Fig C

Fig D

Fig E

Fig F

Fig G

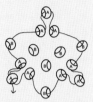

Fig H

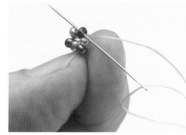

Extension rope step 2

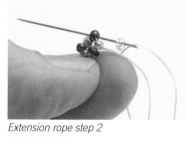

Extension rope step 2

Extension rope step 2

Extension rope step 2 step up

Extension rope step 3a

Extension rope step 3b

Extension rope step 5a

Step 5, step up

Extension rope step 12e

Extension rope step 13a

Extension rope step 13b

Extension rope step 13c

Extension rope step 13e

4. Pick up 3B, 3A, the 8-mm round bead), 1B. Turn over the B, and work back up the 8-mm round, 3A and 3B up into the stem, up 3B and around the beads making the loop. Tie to the tail thread and fasten both threads away.

This is a lovely necklace on its own, but you can enhance it still further to make it look like a lariat which is much longer.

Make the extension

1. Repeat steps 1 to 6 of the rope to make another rope that measures 18 cm. End with a B row. You will now start to increase to make the flowers.

2. Increase row: Pick up 2A together and through B (3 times) and step up through 1A, splitting the increase (Fig G).

3. Pick up
a. 1A and through the next A (Fig H)
b. 1B and through the next A (Fig H)
Repeat a, b, a, b and step up into A in the row above.

4. Pick up
a. 1A and through B (Fig J)
b. 1A and through A (Fig J)
Repeat a, b, a, b and step up through to the A above (Fig J).

5. Pick up
a. 1B and through A (Fig K)
b. 2A together and through A (Fig K)
Repeat a, b, a, b and step up through B (Fig K).

6. Pick up
a. 1A and through A (splitting the increase – Fig L)
b. 1A and through the next A (in the increase – Fig L)
c. 1A and through B (Fig L)
Repeat a, b, c, a, b, c and step up into the A above.

7. Pick up
a. 1A and through an A
b. 1A and through an A
c. 1B and through A (Fig M)
Repeat a, b, c, a, b, c and step up through A (Fig M).

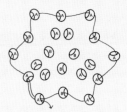

Fig J

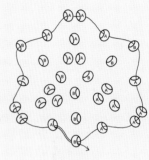

Fig K

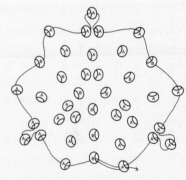

Fig L

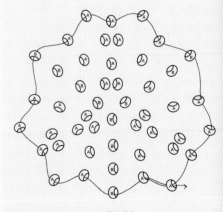

Fig M

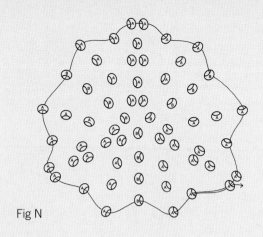

Fig N

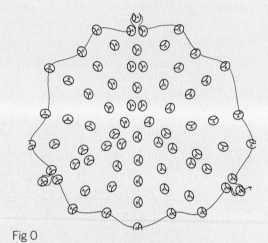

Fig O

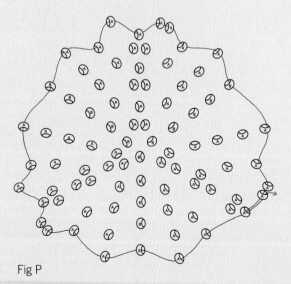

Fig P

8. Pick up

a. 2A together and through A (Fig N)

b. 1A and through B (Fig N)

c. 1A and through A

Repeat a, b, c, a, b, c and step up through 1A (splitting the increase – Fig N).

9. Pick up

a. 1A and through the next A (A sits in between the increase – Fig O)

b. 1A and through A (Fig O)

c. 1B and through A

d. 1A and through A

Repeat a, b, c, b, a, b, c, b an up into A that splits the increase.

10. Pick up

a. 2A together, and through the next A (Fig P)

b. 1A and through B (Fig P)

c. 1A and through A (Fig P)

Repeat a, c, b, c, c, a, b, a, c and step up through 1A, the first bead in the increase.

11. Pick up

a. 1A, and through A (the A sits between the increase beads – Fig Q)

b. 1A and through A

c. 1B and through A

d. 1A and through A (needle goes through the first A of the increase) Repeat a, b, b, c, b, d, a, b, c, b, d and step up through A.

12. Pick up

a. 1A and through A

b. 1A and through B

c. 1A and through A

d. 1A and through A

e. 2A and through A

Repeat a to e two more times and step up through A.

13. Now use the 14° seed beads (F) to neaten the top of the flower. Pick up

a. 2F and through A

b. 1B and through A

c. 2F and through A

d. 2F and through A

e. 1F and through A (F will sit in between the increase)

f. 2F and through A

Repeat a, b, c, d, e, f, a, b, c, d, e, f

14. You've completed the flower top; now work your way down to the base of the flower on the B line and go through to the inside of the flower at the base (Fig U).

a. Thread on 12C and a drop. Turn back up the 12C beads and through the B line back to the outside of the flower; work your way to the next B line and go through to the inside.

b. Pick up 11C and a drop. Turn back up the 11C beads and through the B line back to the outside of the flower; work your way to the third B line, and through to the inside

c. Pick up 13C and a drop. Turn back up the 13C beads and through the B line to the outside of the flower. Work your thread away.

Do the same on the other end of the extension. Tie the extension into the rope as shown.

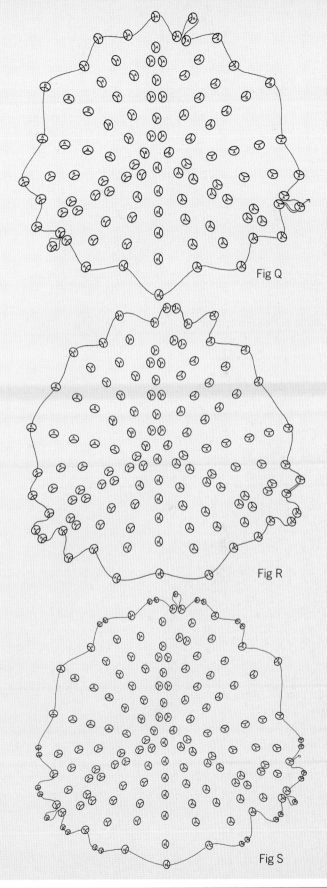

Fig Q

Fig R

Fig S

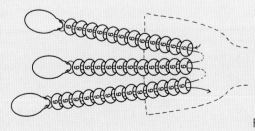

Fig T

Simone necklace

For this lovely piece you will again use even-count tubular peyote, but the colour arrangement differs from that of Cindy, and it is heavily embellished. It is a good choice to wear in the evening, as it uses a combination of mixed beads and fire crystals. It would be even more striking if you used crystal bicones. I have kept all the beads for embellishment to 4 mm, or as close as possible, as the necklace is on the long side to be worn over a garment. Bigger beads would have made it too heavy, but remain an alternative. The inner tube with a focal centre piece would also look nice on its own. To keep it looking delicate to go with the crystals, I used 11º seed beads, hence the tube does not grow as quickly as the Cindy rope, but the colour palette is vast in this range and I feel it was well worth it. The necklace measures 61 cm without the clasp.

You will need

2200A 11° seed beads (light)
2200B 11° seed beads (med)
700C 11° seed beads (darker)
300L 11° seed beads (neutral – silver)
26D 5° triangles (light)
26J 5° triangles (darker)
26E 4-mm drops (Japanese light)
26K 4-mm drops (Japanese med)
26F 4-mm crystal bicones (light)
26G 4-mm facetted crystals (light as A)
26H 4-mm facetted crystals (med as B)
26I 4-mm facetted crystals (dark as C)
Clasp
Nymo B thread
#11 beading needle

Tube

1. Thread up with about 2,25 m, pick up 1A, 1B, 1A, 1B, 1A, 1B, take the beads down the thread leaving a tail of about 30 cm and tie a reef knot. Take the needle through the first bead to the left – the A bead (Fig A).

2. Pick up 1B and miss a B and through the next A (Fig B).

3. Pick up 1B and miss a B and through the next A.

4. Pick up 1B and miss a B and through the next A.

5. Now take the needle and thread up through the next B, the first B of the new row (we call this stepping up). You will have 3B beads sitting on top of your first row.

6. Pick up 1A and through the next B, repeat two more times, then step up through A (Fig C). You will have 3A beads on the top

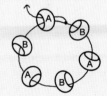

Fig A

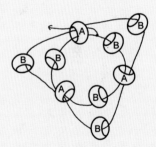

Fig B

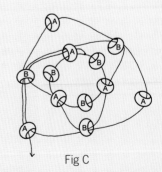

Fig C

7. Repeat steps 2 to 6 until your tube is long enough. Picking up 3A or 3B for each row, I made mine 61cm, long.

Loop embellishments

The tube makes a lovely necklace on its own, but can be further embellished by working around it in a spiral. Fasten a new length of thread into the end of the tube coming out of the B bead, needle pointing to the left, the end on top (Fig D).

1. Loop in B

a. Pick up 6B, miss a B and go down through the next B in the straight line of B. I now hold the tube with the end towards the right, so my needle comes down towards me with the length of the tube on my left (Fig E). You have made your first loop. The necklace is made up of loops, and you will now get the needle and thread back to the right place for the next loop.

b. Turn and go back through the B bead below (to the left of) the one you came through to finish your loop (Fig F). Shunt forward into the A stripe, one up (or third bead from the top) – to the left if the end is at the top (Fig G).

c. Turn back through the second A bead from the top (Fig H).

d. Turn again and work through the first A bead in the row, needle out on the left, (holding top up) ready for the next pick up. You have made a Z with your thread (Fig J).

2. Loop in B

a. Pick up 6B, miss an A and through the next A (the third A bead down) needle pointing towards the right (or towards you if the end is on the right). Your new loop sits in front of the first loop. You will build the loops around the rope – the next will be in front of the second loop (Fig K).

b. Turn and go back through the A bead below the one you have just gone through as in step 1b (Fig F). Shunt forward into the B stripe, one up (or fourth bead from the top) as Fig G towards the left.

c. Turn back through the third B from the top as in Fig H.

d. Turn again and through the second B bead, needle out on the left, ready for the next pick-up (Fig L).

3. Loop in A

a. Pick up 6A, miss a B and through the next B as in Fig E.

b. Turn and go back through the B bead below as in Fig F. Shunt forward into the A stripe, one up (or fourth bead from the top) as in Fig G.

c. Turn and back through the A bead above as in Fig H.

d. Turn again and through the A bead above, having made your Z (second bead from the top), as in Fig J.

Fig D

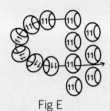

Fig E

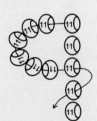

Fig F

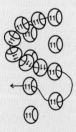

Fig G

Part 3

STEP	PICK UP	HEADER	LOOP
1	6B	no	complete
2	6A	no	complete
3	3C	1D	3C and complete
4	6A	no	complete
5	6B	no	complete
6	6B	no	complete
7	1A	1L, 1E, turn, back through 1L	1A and complete
8	6C	no	complete
9	6A	no	complete
10	2B	1F, 1L, turn, back through 1F	2B and complete
11	6B	no	complete
12	6A	no	complete
13	6C	no	complete
14	2A	1G, 1L, turn, back through 1G	2A and complete
15	6B	no	complete
16	6B	no	complete
17	2A	1H, 1L, turn, back through 1H	2A and complete
18	6C	no	complete
19	6A	no	complete
20	6B	no	complete
21	2B	1I, 1L, turn, back through 1I	2B and complete
22	6A	no	complete
23	6C	no	complete
24	3A	1J	3A and complete
25	6B	no	complete
26	6B	no	complete
27	6A	no	complete
28	2C	1K	2C and complete

Following the sequence, start part 4 with A:

Part 4

STEP	PICK UP	HEADER	LOOP
1	6A	no	complete
2	6B	no	complete
3	3B	1D	3B and complete
4	6A	no	complete
5	6C	no	complete
6	6A	no	complete
7	1B	1L, 1E, turn, back through 1L	1B and complete

8	6B	no	complete
9	6A	no	complete
10	2C	1F, 1L, turn, back through 1F	2C and complete
11	6A	no	complete
12	6B	no	complete
13	6B	no	complete
14	2A	1G, 1L, turn, back through 1G	2A and complete
15	6C	no	complete
16	6A	no	complete
17	2B	1H, 1L, turn, back through 1H	2B and complete
18	6B	no	complete
19	6A	no	complete
20	6C	no	complete
21	2A	1I, 1L, turn, back through 1I	2A and complete
22	6B	no	complete
23	6B	no	complete
24	3A	1J	3A and complete
25	6C	no	complete
26	6A	no	complete
27	6B	no	complete
28	2B	1K	2B and complete

Following the sequence, start part 5 with A:

Part 5

STEP	PICK UP	HEADER	LOOP
1	6A	no	complete
2	6C	no	complete
3	3A	1D	3A and complete
4	6B	no	complete
5	6B	no	complete
6	6A	no	complete
7	1C	1L, 1E, turn, back through 1L	1C and complete
8	6A	no	complete
9	6B	no	complete
10	2B	1F, 1L, turn, back through 1E	2B and complete
11	6A	no	complete
12	6C	no	complete
13	6A	no	complete

STEP	PICK UP	HEADER	LOOP
14	2B	1G, 1L, turn, back through 1G	2B and complete
15	6B	no	complete
16	6A	no	complete
17	2C	1H, 1L, turn, back through 1H	2C and complete
18	6A	no	complete
19	6B	no	complete
20	6B	no	complete
21	2A	1I, 1L, turn, back through 1I	2A and complete
22	6C	no	complete
23	6A	no	complete
24	3B	1J	3B and complete
25	6B	no	complete
26	6A	no	complete
27	6C	no	complete
28	2A	1K	2A and complete

Following the sequence, start part 6 with B:

Part 6

STEP	PICK UP	HEADER	LOOP
1	6B	no	complete
2	6B	no	complete
3	3A	1D	3A and complete
4	6C	no	complete
5	6A	no	complete
6	6B	no	complete
7	1B	1L, 1E, turn, back through 1L	1B and complete
8	6A	no	complete
9	6C	no	complete
10	2A	1F, 1L, turn, back through 1F	2A and complete
11	6B	no	complete
12	6B	no	complete
13	6A	no	complete
14	2C	1G, 1L, turn, back through 1G	2C and complete
15	6A	no	complete
16	6B	no	complete
17	2B	1H, 1L, turn, back through 1H	2B and complete
18	6A	no	complete

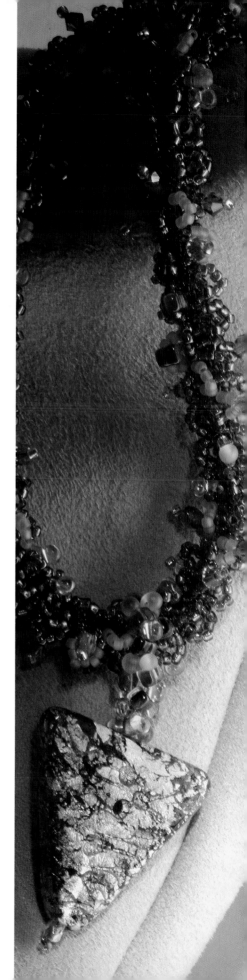

19	6C	no	complete
20	6A	no	complete
21	2B	1I, 1L, turn, back through 1I	2B and complete
22	6B	no	complete
23	6A	no	complete
24	3C	1J	3C and complete
25	6A	no	complete
26	6B	no	complete
27	6B	no	complete
28	2A	1K	2A and complete

Repeat parts 2 to 6 twice, then repeat parts 2 and 3 again. You would have completed 18 rounds of loops with headers. Repeat part 4, steps 1 to 21, or continue until you have only six empty beads left at the end of the line to the top. Carry on working these beads with the loops with no header, but keep the colour sequence going until the last loop falls into the last bead of the line.

Clasps

Go around the three proud beads (the beads that are higher) twice, and pull up tight, then pick up 3B, clasp, 3B, and enter one of the proud beads on the other side of the tube (Fig P). Repeat the fastening again to strengthen, and fasten off by knotting twice and travelling. Do the same on the other side.

Optional focal bead

I added a focal bead in much the same way as I did the tassel for the Cindy necklace, only it was just one bead. So make a ring around the rope, loosely (see page 69 – I used triangles and drops), and then take your needle down the big bead to the base, turn and back up to the ring, knot and repeat. This can slip on and off.

Simone chunky

You can also make Simone very chunky. Make the tube the same as for Simone. For the embellishments, make the loops the same as for Simone, but put larger size header on to each loop. I used seven different beads ranging from a 6° seed bead to a 8-mm shaped bead. I also used chips. These will make the necklace heavier, so it is better worn short (see photographs on pages 80-81).

Katinka necklace

For this unusual necklace you will also use even-count tubular peyote, increasing and decreasing within your work at the beginning and at the end of the tubes. It is made up of tubes made from smaller beads, made into a big bead. The beauty of this is that whatever the colour of your outfit, there will always be beads to match, and by "beading your own beads" there is very little likelihood of someone else having the same combination. You can even mix the colour in one necklace, and if you assemble the made beads differently you can create a different look altogether.

Combining the made beads with chain work which is so popular at the moment, gives the necklace a more earthy look. The necklace is worn long, but you can shorten the chain at the back and have a short necklace as well. With it being long, I like to combine it with another piece of chain, with matching beads attached, worn short. The little chain is also sweet on its own.

10. Pick up

a.   1C, miss an A and through an A.

b.   1A, miss a D and through a D.

c.   1D, miss an F and through an E.

d.   1E, miss a G and through a G.

e.   1A, miss an E and through an E.

f.   1A, miss a B and through a B.

g.   1A, miss a B and through a C.

Step 5c

Step 5d

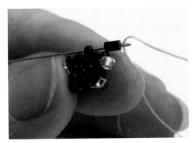

Step 5e

Step 5f

Step 5g

Step 6a

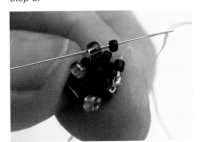

Step 6b

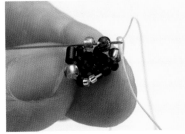

Step 6e

Step 9

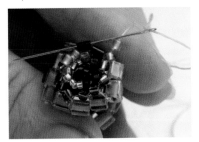

Step 10d

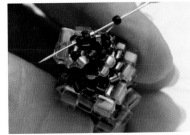

Step 11b

Step 13

11. Pick up

a. 1C miss an A and through an A

b. 1A miss a D and through a D

c. 1A miss an E and through an E

d. An A miss a G and through an A

e. An A miss an E and through an A

f. An A miss a B and through an A

g. An A through C, plus A, and next up A

12 Work another round all in A adding 6 A beads. Go through two beads, pick up 1A and through the next A (3 times – 3 beads).

13. Take the thread around the 3 beads twice, and end off, by knotting and travelling twice. These are your long beads. Make four long ones to be used around the neck. Then make one shorter bead, putting in only 20F beads, and finish as the above beads. This will be the bead hanging down the front.

Assemble the necklace (Fig D)

1. Start with the shortest bead that will sit at the front with the tassel hanging from it. Cut a piece of wire 4 cm longer than the made bead, and turn a wire-chain loop (see page 22) on one end. Thread on one H square bead and carefully place your made bead onto the wire (careful not to snag the thread), followed by another H bead, and turn another wire-chain loop on the other side. Repeat with all the made beads.

2. Cut a piece of chain with six links (you will cut in the seventh link as that one will fall away). Open a jump ring with two pairs of pliers, holding the jump ring on either side, pulling one towards you and one away from you, until you have a small gap to insert the chain and the loop. Close the jump ring pulling in the opposite direction. The bead and chain will be linked. Repeat to link the pieces.

3. Take a 6-mm round bead J, make a wire-chain loop with a head pin (see page 22) and connect to the chain in the last link with a jump ring. Using another head pin, place another 6-mm round I bead in the next link up, the last 6-mm round J bead in the second link from the top with a head pin. Place a leaf into the jump ring that connects the chain to the made bead.

4. Cut two more pieces of chain with nine links (cut in the tenth link) and use the jump ring to connect both pieces of chain with the loop from the made short, and close.

5. Join to a made bead, (second bead up) one for each chain. Cut another piece of chain with nine links and join to the top of the bead with a jump ring.

Fig D

6. Join to a made bead (third bead up) one on either side. Gauge how long you want to make your necklace and cut. I cut my chain 20 cm, joined with a jump ring, and on the other side I attached a clasp with a jump ring. Your necklace now only needs embellishment.

7. I staggered my beads that were all put on with jump rings and wrapped-chain loops. The leaves all go on the outside of the chain; the beads go on both the outside and the inside.

a. First piece of chain side 1: 2nd link (from tassel) 1x6-mm I bead inside of link; 5th link up 1x6-mm J bead, outside; 7th link leaf outside.

b. First piece of chain side 2: 3rd link 1x 6-mm J bead, outside; 6th link up 1x 6-mm I bead, inside; 9th link up 1 leaf, outside. You are now at the 2nd bead.

c. Middle piece of chain side 1: 3rd link up 1x6-mm I bead, outside; 6th link up 1x6-mm J bead inside; 9th link outside, leaf.

d. Middle piece of chain side 2: 2nd link 1x6-mm J bead, outside; 5th link 1x 6-mm I bead inside; 7th link up, leaf outside.

e. Mirror the pattern on the chain above the last bead, just up to the 9th link. The rest is left as a chain, but should you wish to embellish it, then do.

Optional short chain

Cut another piece of chain 48 cm long, and place a J bead in the middle link, working towards the clasp. Miss two links and place an I bead on either side of the J bead, miss 2 links again and place another J. I put on 11 beads and wear the two chains together.

Michelle necklace

This interesting necklace is made using even-count tubular peyote. I increased and decreased within the tube to create the twist. It is a little more advanced than some of the other projects, but as I have already covered the basics in *Dare to bead* I wanted to lead you on to a little more of a challenge. I used soft wire in the middle of the tube so that I could use the entire length as a bead, and broke it up with large made beads and large jump rings. It is finished off with a tassel made with wire, using all the wire techniques covered in the previous section.

The necklace was designed to be worn with the tassel in the front, but the catch can be removed, and I suggest you buy two catches so that you can also wear it short with the long twisted section in the front, caught at the back with the spare catch through two of the rings nearer to the beading. This technique also makes a lovely bracelet (seep page 103). Simply add a suitable fastener.

The tassel is made up with all of the larger beads used in the necklace plus a few extra. Make an extra tassel and attach it to your handbag as well to match. Have fun.

Fig N

Fig O

Fig P

a. Gently take the wire through one large jump ring, and back over itself through the crimp, the H and the J beads, and gently pull tight (you have made a loop with the jump ring attached) (Fig N).

b. Squash the crimp bead, place a little glue at the end of the J bead and cut the wire (Fig O).

12. Do the same on the other side, taking special care to feed the wire through gently to tighten it without making any kinks. Assemble all the made beads in this way.

13. Assemble the large and the small made beads. Take two small jump rings, open them and put them onto the ring at the end of the made beads. Insert another large jump ring and close the small jump rings – you now have a large jump ring and another large jump ring held together with two small jump rings (Fig P).

14. Place two more small jump rings onto the last large jump ring and insert the large jump ring at the end of the small made bead, close the small jump rings. Do the same on the other side.

15. Place two more small jump rings plus the big jump ring on the other side of the small made beads and close the small jump rings.

Tassel

The tassel also makes a lovely hand bag decoration or key ring.

Smaller bead step 6d

Smaller bead step 6f

Smaller bead step 6g

Smaller bead step 7h

Smaller bead step 7h up 1D 1A

Insert wire to continue

Smaller bead step 9e

Smaller bead step 9f

Smaller bead step 9g

Smaller bead step 10a

Smaller bead step 10b

Smaller bead step 10f

peyote stitch 101

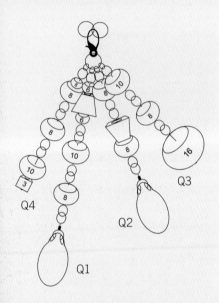

Fig Q

The bracelet on the opposite page was made using the same technique as for the made beads of the necklace.

1. Make the first drop (Fig Q1).

a. Start with a leaf or drop, and make a wrapped loop from a drop (see page 25).

b. Make a wire-chain loop on each side of a 8mm round bead, connecting it to this leaf or drop.

c. Make a wire-chain loop on each side of a 10-mm round bead, and connect to the result of b.

d. Make a wire-chain loop on a piece of wire and place on a shaped bead plus 1E bead, and make a wire chain loop, attach to the result of c.

e. Insert a 6-mm jump ring into the loop.

2. Second drop (Fig Q2).

a. Start with a leaf or drop, and make a wrapped loop from a drop.

b. Make a wire-chain loop on each side of a 8-mm round bead and a shaped bead and make another wire-chain loop on the top, connecting it to this leaf or drop

c. Make a wire chain loop on each side of another 8-mm bead and connect to the result of b.

d. Insert a 6-mm jump ring into the loop.

3. Third drop (Fig Q3).

a. Start with a headpin, place on 1E and the 16-mm round bead, and bend a wire-chain loop.

b. Make a wire-chain loop on either side of an 8-mm bead, and connect to the result of a.

c. Make a wire-chain loop on each side of the 10-mm round bead and connect to the result of b.

d. Make a wire-chain loop on each side of an 8-mm round bead and attach to the result of c.

e. Insert a small jump ring into the loop.

4. Fourth drop (Fig Q4).

a. Start with a headpin and place on 1F, followed by 1J and make a wire-chain loop.

b. Make a wire-chain loop on either side of an 8-mm bead and attach to the result of a.

c. Make a wire-chain loop on one side of a piece of wire, place on an 8-mm bead plus 1D, make a loop and attach to the result of b.

d. Insert a small jump ring, into the loop.

5. Insert a small 6-mm jump ring into the base of the lobster clasp. Take the same jump ring and insert the top jump rings of all four drops into the jump ring at the base of the clasp. Close.

Fig D

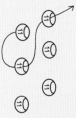

Fig E

Fig F

Shape the end

To shape the end, decrease and work in odd-count peyote.

1. Work 1 more row all in A, six times, then turn back deur the D bead, and take your thread between the As and deur the first A (Fig D).

2. Peyote 5A, turn as above (Fig E).

3. Peyote 4A, turn as above (Fig F).

4. Peyote 3A, turn as above (Fig E).

5. Peyote 2A, turn as above (Fig F).

6. Peyote 1A, turn (Fig G).

7. Take your needle back deur the A bead. Pick up 1 round 8-mm, plus 1A, go back over the A and deur the 8-mm and into the other side of the A. (Fig H). Repeat to strengthen and then work your thread back into the body of the bracelet.

Make the loop for the button, and edge

1. Remove the stop bead and thread up with a nice long thread. Fasten into you work, ending with the needle deur the two end beads facing in towards the centre.

2. Peyote 5A, as in step 2 for shaping, then peyote 4A as in step 3 left, peyote 3A as in step 4 left, 2A, and lastly 1A.

3. Turn and come out of the top A bead, pick up 18A and go back deur the other side of the A bead (Fig J).

4. Now peyote into the 18 ring-beads to broaden the loop, putting in 9A beads. Turn and go back deur the loop, weaving to strengthen. If you find this loop a little on the loose side, you can put an extra bead on the inside of the loop where it joins the bracelet (Fig K).

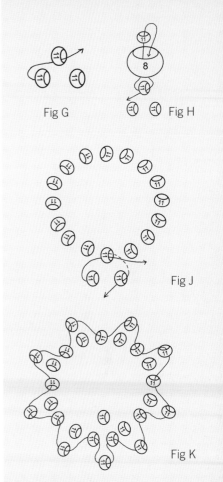

Fig G

Fig H

Fig J

Fig K

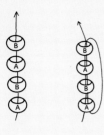

Fig A   Fig B

Fig C

Fig D

Fig E

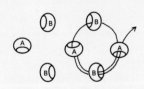

Fig F

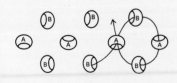

Fig G

Right-angle weave

Right angle weave is one of the more interesting stitches for off-loom beading, as there are beads facing north, south, east, and west in any one given stitch. So it makes shaping much easier as you can go off into angles, which makes it a very versatile stitch. It also makes a lovely soft fabric, as you will see in this section. It is softer than the peyote or brick (covered in *Dare to bead*) and adapts very well when used in conjunction with peyote stitch. The beads will convert very well from one stitch to the other. Though the conventional right-angle weave is made up of four beads, one at the top, one at the bottom and one on either side, it can easily be changed to eight or even 12, or having unequal sides, say two each at the top and bottom, and one on either side (six beads) as you will see when you make Isobel (see page 114). The thread always comes out of one side into the other making right angles, hence the name.

Flat right-angle weave

Work with four beads, foundation row in two colours:

1. Pick up four beads, A, B, A, B, and take them down your thread (Fig A). Go back up all four beads again, in a clockwise motion from the tail side, and pull tight to form a little box (Fig C). The thread comes out of B, now take it on up, still in a clockwise motion, through A,B,A (Fig D). We will call this A bead your leader bead. The leader bead will change with each right-angle stitch. It points in the direction you are to work in, and you will always start from the old leader bead and end up in the new leader bead.

2. Now pick up another three beads, B, A, B. One bead of the right angle is already there. The thread comes out of the **bottom** of the A bead – the old leader bead (Fig E). Join it by going down the old leader in an anti-clock wise motion. Pull up. Continue on around through B, and up A (the new leader bead). You now have two right angles (Fig F).

3. Pick up another three beads, B, A, B (Fig G). One bead to the right angle is already there. The thread comes out of the **top** of the A bead (the old leader

bead). Join it by going up the old leader, in a clockwise motion. Pull up. Continue on around through B, and down A (the new leader bead). You now have three right angles.

4. Repeat steps 2 and 3 for as long as you need.

Weave a fabric

To weave a fabric off the foundation row, the thread comes out of the A bead (the old leader). Now you will change the leader. Remember, the leader points in the direction in which you will be working. You need to go down, so the B bead will become the leader. As you always start from the leader, take the needle on around through the B bead (Fig J).

1. Pick up three beads A,B,A. One bead to the right angle is already there. The thread comes out to the left of the B bead (the old leader) (Fig K). Join it by going through the old leader in an anti-clock wise motion. Pull up. Continue through one more A bead which will now become your new leader, pointing in the direction in which you will be working (Fig L).

2. I like to turn my work so that I am working from left to right. The thread comes down, out of the A bead (the old leader). Pick up only two more beads B,A. Two beads to the right angle are already there (Fig M). Join it by going through the bottom B bead of the right angle in the top row, and then down through the A bead in the new row (the old leader) in an ant- clock wise motion. Then continue on up to the new leader, through two beads B, A (Fig N). You now have two right angles.

3. The thread is up out of the A bead (the leader), so you will join it first, through the bottom B bead of the right angle of the first row (Fig O). Pick up two more beads A, B. Two beads to the right angle are already there (Fig P). Join it by going up the old leader A bead in a clockwise motion, and through two more beads, B, A, to the new leader (Fig Q).

Fig H

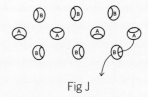

Fig J

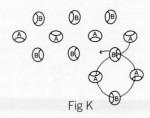

Fig K

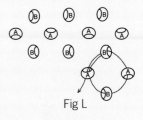

Fig L

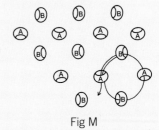

Fig M

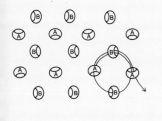

Fig Q

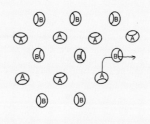

Fig P

Fig O

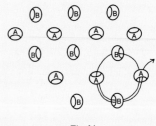

Fig N

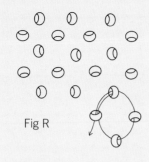

Fig R

Fig S

Fig T

Fig U

Fig V

Fig Y

4. Repeat steps 2 and 3 for the body and then go back to step 1 to start a new row. Remember, the leader will always be in the direction you are working and the thread always ends through the leader. Pick up three beads for the start of a new row (second, third and so on), two beads having already started, as two beads are already there (Fig R).

Combinations

Right-angle weave can be used with many different combinations:

- The conventional four beads (Fig S).
- Eight beads with the same number of beads in all the sides (Fig T).
- Twelve beads with the same number of beads in all the sides (Fig U).
- Then one can change the combinations, for example six (Fig V).
- Eight beads with different sides (Fig Y).

Right-angle weave with two needles

Although it takes a little getting used to, right-angle weave can also be worked with two needles.

1. Thread a needle on to each end of a length of thread. Pick up a bead and centre it on the thread (Fig A).

2. Pick up another bead with each needle (Fig B).

3. Pick up one more bead onto the left-hand needle; take it just beyond the needle, and over your finger (Fig C).

4. Take the right-hand needle through the same bead, going in where the first needle came out, crossing the threads in the bead (Fig D).

5. Now take a needle in each hand and pull, until the beads are in the middle of the thread, forming a right angle (Fig E).

6. Repeat steps 2 tot 5 for as long as you need.

Increasing

1. To increase at the end you have to make an extra stitch (Fig F).

2. To increase in the beginning, you also make an extra stitch. Finish your row and make the first stitch as normal (Fig G). After joining, go on around two more beads to the edge, and add another right angle (Fig H). After joining,

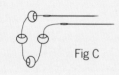

Fig A

Fig B

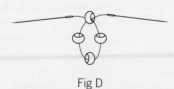

Fig C

Fig D

work through the one right angle (the first one) to the new leader, and continue (Figs I and J).

3. Increasing in the body of the work can either be in the first row, or well into the fabric.

a. To increase in the first row, pick up four beads and attach. You will have one bead at the top, one at the side, and two at the bottom, and the beads will split, giving you a right angle. (Fig K).

b. To increase well into the fabric. Bring the thread out of the bottom of the side bead and pick up three beads, two for the bottom, and one for the other side, before joining to the top (Fig L). The beads will split, each into its own right angle (Fig M).

Decreasing

1. To decrease at the end, just make one stitch less at the end (Fig N).

2. To decrease in the beginning, work your way over one right angle and start at the second (Fig O).

3. To decrease in the body of the work, when attaching a new right angle go through two beads (attach to two right angles); they will become one (Fig P).

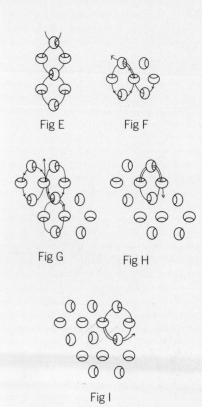

Fig E   Fig F

Fig G   Fig H

Fig I

Fig J

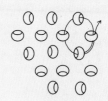

Fig M

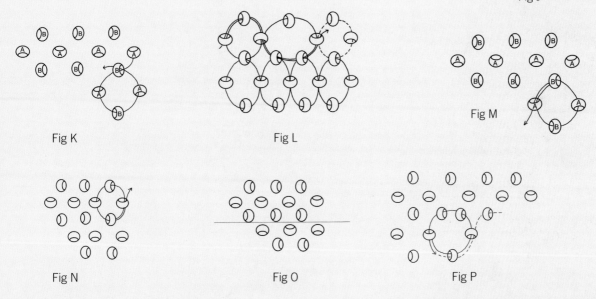

Fig K   Fig L

Fig N   Fig O   Fig P

Isobel necklace

An eye-catching piece made up using many different combinations of different numbers of beads in the right-angle weave. It is a good piece for you to become familiar with the stitch. I included beads of many different sizes to show you the effect. With the small beads using just chain is most effective. This has then been broken up and a large bead inserted. There are three chains to this piece. If you don't want to make that many, just leave one out. It is important that you use glass beads to give this piece weight, or it will not hang well.

You will need

For chain 1 (shortest chain)
250A 11º seed beads (main colour)
80B 11º seed beads (second colour)
60C 11º seed beads (third colour)
80D 15º seed beads (same as C)
30E 4-mm round beads (main colour)
7F 6-mm round crystals
8G 8-mm round pearls
2x6-mm jump rings
For chain 2 (middle chain)
320A 11º seed beads (main colour)
80B 11º seed beads (second colour)
40C 11º seed beads (third colour)
90C 15º seed beads (same as C)
35E 4-mm round pearls
24F 6-mm round crystals
9G 8-mm round pearls
5H 12-mm round crystals
2x6-mm jump rings 2
For chain 3 (longest chain)
400A 11º seed beads (main colour)
100B 11º seed beads (second colour)
50C 11º seed beads (third colour)
95D 15º seed beads (same as C)
40E 4-mm round pearls
25F 6-mm round crystals
9G 8-mm round pearls
5H 12-mm round crystals
1x22x25-mm brass heart
2x6-mm jump rings
Toggle clasp
Nymo B thread
#11 beading needle

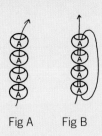

Fig A   Fig B

Fig C

Fig D

Fig E

Fig F

Fig G

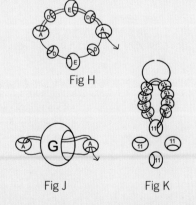

Fig H

Fig J   Fig K

Make the short chain

1. Pick up 4A and take them down the thread (Fig A), leaving about 30 cm. Go back up the 4A from the tail-side up (Fig B). Bring the beads into a circle and then on around 3 more beads (one right angle – Fig C). The bead farthest to the right pointing in the direction you will work is the leader bead (see page 110), the bead your thread comes out of.

2. Pick up 1B, 1A, 1B (3 beads, as one bead is already there), join to the leader in an anti-clockwise motion (Fig D), and then go on around two more beads (Fig E). This will be your new leader (two right angles).

3. Pick up 3A (three beads, as one is already there), join to the leader in a clockwise motion (Fig F), and then go on around two more beads (Fig G). This will be your new leader (right angle no 3).

Continue in this manner repeating the method in rows 2 and 3 (note that the beads in row 2 are joined in an anti-clock wise and in row 3 in a clockwise motion). These two rows will form the foundation chain, following the pick up combination below:

ROW	PICK UP	JOIN
4	1B, 1A, 1B	anti-clockwise
5	3A	clockwise
6	3A	anti-clockwise
7	1B, 1A, 1B	clockwise
8	3A	anti-clockwise
9	1B, 1A, 1B	clockwise
10	3A	anti-clockwise
11	1C, 1A, 1C	clockwise
12	1D, 1E, 1D, 1A, 1D, 1E, 1D	To the A, around 4 more beads, D, E, D, A and continue (Fig H)
13	1C, 1A, 1C	clockwise
14	3A	anti-clockwise
15	1B, 1A, 1B	clockwise
16	3A	anti-clockwise
17	1B, 1A, 1B	clockwise
18	3A	anti-clockwise

19 BEAD BREAK: take your needle through the G bead and pick up 1A, go over the A, back through G, and into the other side of the other A, through G again and A (Fig J).

20 Repeat rows 6 to 12 inclusive.

27 BEAD BREAK: take your needle through the F bead and pick up 1A, go over the A, back through F, and into the other side of the other A, through F again and A.

28 Repeat rows 12 to 19 (taking you to row 35), then rows 6 to 13, taking you to row 43.

44 BEAD BREAK: take your needle through the G bead and pick up 1A, go over the A, back through G, and into the other side of the other A, through G again and A (Fig J).

45 Repeat rows 11 to 19 (taking you to row 53) then rows 6 to 13 (taking you to row 61).

62 BEAD BREAK: as for row 27.

63 Repeat rows 11 to 19 (taking you to row 71). This is half way. Work the other half to match.

Work the ends

Pick up 8D, thread through a jump ring and back around the right angle, repeat to strengthen (Fig K). Repeat on the other side using the tail thread. I prefer to go back to the other side through all the right angles to strengthen the chain, then knot and travel, and knot again.

Make the middle chain

1. Pick up 4A, take them down your thread leaving a tail of about 30 cm (Fig A), pass the needle up the same 4A again from the tail-side up (Fig B), bring the beads into a circle, and then go on around another 3 beads (Fig C). The bead the thread comes out of is the leader bead.

2. Pick up 1B, 1A, 1B, (3 beads), as one bead is already there, join to the leader in an anti-clockwise motion (Fig D), and then go on around two more beads to the new leader (Fig E) (2 right angles).

3. Pick up 3A (3 beads), as one is already there, join to the leader in a clockwise motion (Fig F), and then go on around 2 more beads (Fig G). This will be your new leader (right angle no 3).

Continue in this manner repeating the method in rows 2 and 3 to form the foundation chain, following the pick up combination below:

ROW	PICK UP	JOIN
4	1B, 1A, 1B	anti-clockwise
5	3A	clockwise
6	1C, 1A, 1C	anti-clockwise
7	1D, 1E, 1D, 1A, 1D, 1E, 1D	to A, around 4 more beads D, E, D, and A then continue (Fig H)
8	1C, 1A, 1C	anti-clockwise
9	3A	clockwise
10	1B, 1A, 1B	anti-clockwise
11	3A	clockwise
12	1B, 1A, 1B	anti-clockwise
13	3A	clockwise
14	BEAD BREAK: Take your needle through the G bead, pick up 1A, go over the A bead and back through G, through the other side of the first A, and back through G and A (Fig J).	
15	3A	clockwise
16	1B, 1A, 1B	anti-clockwise
17	3A	clockwise
18	1B, 1A, 1B	anti-clockwise
19	3A	clockwise
20	1C, 1A, 1C	anti-clockwise
21	1D, 1E, 1D, 1A, 1D, 1E, 1D	to the leader (A), around 4 more beads to the new leader D, E, D, A
22	1A, 1F, 3A, 1F, 1A	to the leader (A), on around through A, F, 2A, to the new leader

23 Repeat rows 7 to 22 inclusive (taking you to row 38).

39 BEAD BREAK: Take your needle through the H bead and pick up 1A, go over the A bead and through H, through the other side of the first A, and turn back through H and A.

40 Repeat row 22.

41 Repeat rows 7 to 22 inclusive, taking you to row 56.

57 BEAD BREAK: repeat row 39.

58 Repeat row 22.

59 Repeat rows 7 to 22 inclusive, taking you to row 74.

75 BEAD BREAK: repeat row 39. This is half way. Work other half to match.

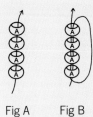

Fig A   Fig B

Fig C   leader

Fig D

Fig E

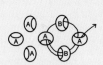

Fig F

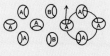

Fig G

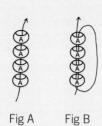

Fig A   Fig B

Fig C

Fig D

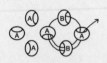

Fig E

Fig F

Fig G

Work the ends

When you have made the last right angle in As, pick up 8D, pass them through the jump ring and back into the right angle, and repeat the thread path to strengthen. Do the same on the other side, then knot travel and knot again.

Make the long chain

1. Pick up 4A, take them down the thread leaving a tail of about 30 cm (Fig A), pass the needle through the same beads again from the tail-side up (Fig B), bring the beads into a circle, and go on around another 3 beads (Fig C). The bead the thread comes out of is the leader bead.

2. Pick up IB, 1A, 1B (3 beads) as one bead is already there (Fig D), and in an anti-clock wise motion join to the leader by going through the A bead, from top to bottom, and then on around 2 more beads (Fig E). This will be your new leader (2 right angles).

3. Pick up 3A (3 beads), as one is already there (Fig F), and in a clockwise motion join to the A bead,(the leader) and then on around 2 more beads (Fig G). This will be your new leader (3 right angles).

Continue in this manner repeating the method in rows 2 and 3 (note that the beads in row 2 are joined in an anti-clock wise and in row 3 in a clockwise motion). These two rows will form the foundation chain, following the pick up combination below:

ROW	PICK-UP	JOIN
4	1B, 1A, 1B	anti-clockwise
5	3A	clockwise
6	1C, 1A, 1C	anti-clockwise
7	1D, 1E, 1D, 1A, 1D, 1E, 1D	To the A, then on around through 4 more beads, D, E, D, A
8	1C, 1A, 1C	anti-clockwise
9	3A	clockwise
10	1B, 1A, 1B	anti-clockwise
11	3A	clockwise
12	1B, 1A, 1B	anti-clockwise
13	3A	clockwise

14 BEAD BREAK: pick up 1E, 1A, take the needle over the A, back through E and through A, turn again and back through E and A.

15 Repeat rows 9 tot 13 inclusive, taking you to row 19.

20 Repeat rows 7 to 13 inclusive, taking you to row 26.

27 BEAD BREAK: pick up 1G, 1A, take the needle over the A and back through the G bead and through the other A. Turn again and through G and A.

28 Repeat rows 9 to 13 inclusive, taking you to row 32.

33 Repeat row 8.

34 Repeat row 7.

35 Pick up 1A, 1F, 3A, 1F, 1A, join to the leader (A) and go on around through 4 more beads A, F, A, A.

36 Repeat row 7.

37 Repeat rows 8 to 13 inclusive, taking you to row 43.

44 BEAD BREAK: Repeat row 27.

45 Repeat rows 9 to 13, taking you to row 49.

50 Repeat row 8.

51 Repeat row 7.

52 Repeat row 35.

53 BEAD BREAK: pick up 1H, 1A, take the needle over the A and back through H and through A on the other side., Turn again and through H and A.

54 Repeat row 35.

55 Repeat rows 7 to-13 inclusive, taking you to row 61.

62 Bead break G: Repeat row 27.

63 Repeat rows 9 to 13 inclusive, taking you to row 67.

68 Repeat row 8.

69 Repeat row 7.

70 Repeat row 35.

Fig H

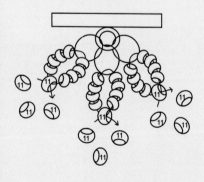

Fig J

71 Bead break H: repeat row 53.

72 Repeat row 35.

73 Repeat rows 7 to 13, taking you to row 79.

80 Bead break G: repeat row 27.

81 Repeat rows 9 to 13, taking you to row 85.

86 Repeat row 8.

87 Repeat row 7.

88 Repeat row 35.

89 Repeat row 53. This is half-way. Work the other half to match, then work the thread back to strengthen the chain. When you get half-way, add the heart.

Add the heart

Having completed row 88 (the row 35 right angle), pick up 7A, 1E, 5A, thread on the heart, pick up another 5A, go back through the E bead, pick up another 7A, and through the big H bead. Repeat three or four times, sometimes going through the leader beads as well, and then continue up the other side to strengthen (Fig H).

Put on the jump rings

Pick up 8D and the jump ring. Pass the needle back through the right angle and repeat to strengthen. Do the same on the other side, using the tail thread on the other side.

Assemble

Open the jump rings one by one and place them onto the clasp. Close them, taking care not to twist them, the jump ring on the shortest chain first, at the top, then the middle one and lastly the long one (Fig J).

Angela

This necklace is made up with a 12-count even-wall right-angle weave, an interesting and very adaptable stitch. The base consists of right angles that come down to a V, where you increase within our work. You will also decrease on the ends, and then embellish the right angle with crystals and pearls. You can make the base right angles any size in order to house the embellishments. I used fresh-water pearls, and 4-mm round crystals, and I hung a 14-mm bicone crystal as a front focal piece. You may have a special bead to use instead. You could make a pair of earrings to complete the piece, using the same centre drop. Or a bracelet, making a band with four to five rows of right-angle weave, and then embellishing it. I made the base in two colours to make it easier for you to see which wall to connect to. It can be done in one colour. If you do it in two colours, choose colours that are close. I used white and clear, with a very fine Nymo 0 thread as the thread goes through the beads many times.

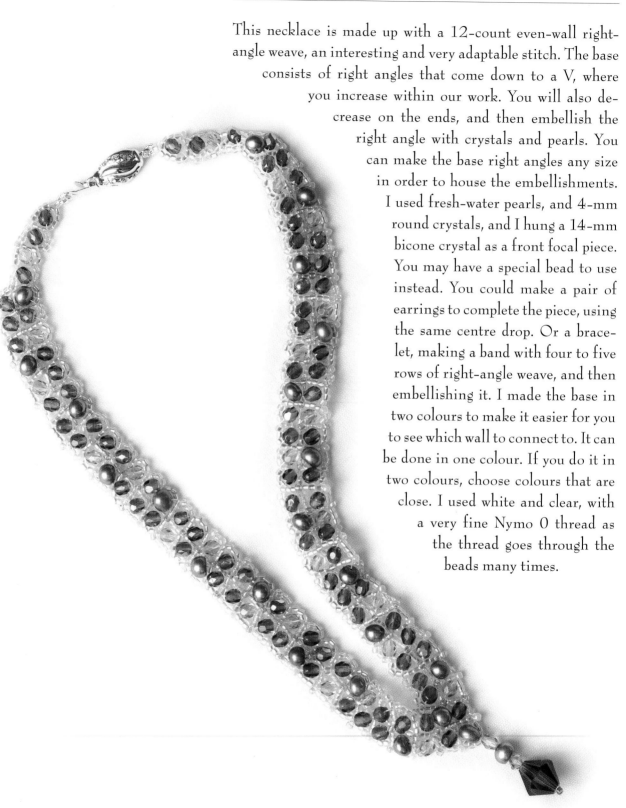

You will need

You will need

10J 15° seed beads (same as main colour)
225A 11° seed beads (main colour)
225B 11° seed beads (very close to main colour)
95C 11° seed beads (second colour)
45D 11° seed beads (third colour)
85E 4-mm round Polish fire crystal (darker)
30F 4-mm round Polish fire crystal (light)
2J 4-mm bicone crystal (same as E)
25G 4-mm fresh-water pearls (tonal to crystals)
1H 14-mm bicone crystal (same as E)
#11 or 12 beading needle or 12.
Nymo beading thread

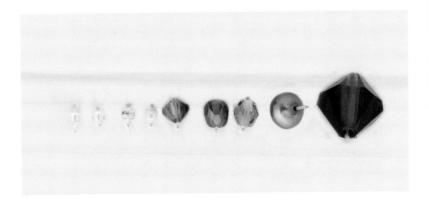

Part 1

1. Start at the back with the inside row. Pick up 12A, and working from left to right, leave a tail of about 20 cm (Fig A). Take the needle up all 12 beads again from the tail-side up, and pull up to form a circle (Fig B). Go on around another 9 beads (both threads are coming out of the bottom – Fig C).

2. Pick up 9B beads, and in an anti-clockwise direction go around and join them down through the 3A beads of the previous right angle (Fig D). Go on around through the first, second and third B beads, and up the fourth, fifth and sixth B beads (Fig E). The thread comes out of the top of the right angle (2 right angles). You will always go on around 6 beads, unless you are changing direction.

3. Pick up 9A and join in a clockwise direction by going up the fourth, fifth, sixth B beads (Fig F), on around the first, second, third, then down the fourth, fifth, sixth A beads (Fig G).

4. Steps 2 and 3 make up the band of right angles (note how one angle is worked in a clockwise direction and the other in an anti-clockwise direction). Repeat them for 33 right angles, or lengthen if necessary, ending on an A square.

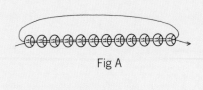

Fig A

Fig B

Fig C

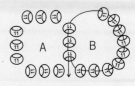

Fig D

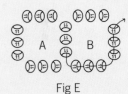

Fig E

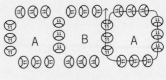

Fig F

Fig G

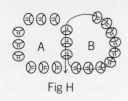

Fig H

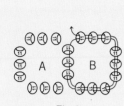

Fig J

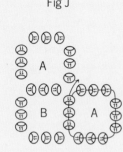

Fig K

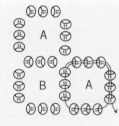

Fig L

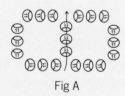

Fig A

Fig B

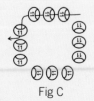

Fig C

5. At the centre right angle, you will end up having changed direction. Pick up 9B and join to the 3A beads (seventh, eighth, ninth beads of the previous right angle – FIG H) and go on around through the first to sixth B beads, then continue through the seventh, eighth and ninth beads. The thread comes out next to the A right angle (Fig J). These 3 beads (seventh, eighth, ninth) are the new leader, 34th square.

6. Continue picking up 9A, and around to join to the 3B beads (Fig K) then on around through the first tot sixth beads, keeping the tension (Fig L). You have formed a V by increasing within your work. That right angle will make 2 right angles on the next row. Continue with steps 2 and 3 until you have made the same number of right angles on the other side to match (33 right angles plus the centre one).

Part 2

1. You will decrease, working from left to right. Put in a new thread to attach the clasp, so needle up the first right angle join (Fig A), knot (Fig B), travel along the top towards the end, knot, and go down 1 bead on the end right angle (Fig C). Pick up 1A, 2J (adjust this according to your clasp) the clasp, 2J and go through 1A and back into the right angle down the last bead (having missed the centre bead – Fig D). Go on around the right angle and up through the clasp again and back into the right angle, then use the tail thread to repeat and strengthen.

2. Work your way to the fourth right angle in on the row, on the joining side to the fifth right angle (you are going to decrease at the beginning of a row). Needle through the base of the fifth right angle and pick up 3B plus 6A, join to the base 3A beads (Fig E) and go on around down the first, second and third B beads in a clockwise direction (Fig F).

3. Pick up 3B plus 3A, (6 beads as you have two sides already there), and as the thread is out of the bottom, join to the base 3 beads in row 1, from right to left, (anti-clockwise – Fig G) and on around down the 3 B side and the 3B base in the new right angle, then up the last side 3A side in the right angle (you have been through 4 sides – Fig H).

4. The thread comes out of the top of the right angle, so you will join straight away in a clock- wise direction, up through the next 3A beads in the right angle in row 1, from left to right (Fig J), then pick up 3B plus 3A (6 beads as 2 sides are already there) and around to join up through the A side of the previous right angle (Fig K), through to the base of row 1 (3A), and down the 3B beads in the new right angle (Fig L).

5. Repeat steps 3 and 4 until you get to the centre (30 right angles).

6. You will make an extra right angle on the end all in A (Fig M). Pick up 9A and join to the A side of the last right angle in the second row (Fig N), and go on around one more side (for you are changing direction) out of the extension (Fig O).

7. For the second side, pick up 3B plus 3A, join to the other half 3B of the centre right angle (Fig P), and continue up three more sides (Fig Q).

8. Continue with step 4 up the second side (Fig R), until you have made 30 right angles to match the first side (plus the centre right angle), leaving four right angles with no second row.

9. Travel on up to the end through these four right angles to attach the other half of the clasp, as in Part 2, step 1.

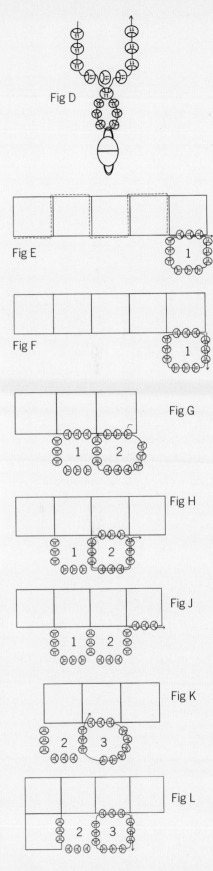

Fig D

Fig E

Fig F

Fig G

Fig H

Fig J

Fig K

Fig L

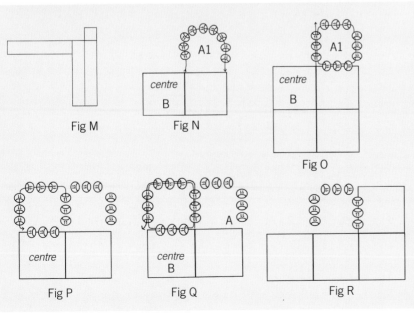

Fig M

Fig N
A1
centre
B

Fig O
A1
centre
B

Fig P
centre

Fig Q
centre
B

Fig R
A

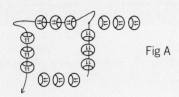

Fig A

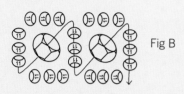

Fig B

Fig C

centre

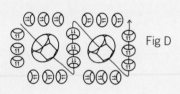

Fig D

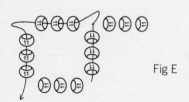

Fig E

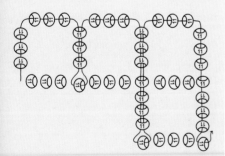

Fig F

Add embellishments

1. Put in a new thread of about 2 m. Come up out of the first right angle, at the join to the second right angle, and knot. Go back the 3 beads to the end and knot and down the next 3 beads (Fig A).

2. Pick up 1E, and lay it diagonally across the right angle, then needle down the 3 beads on the other side so that the crystal lays inside the right angle diagonally (Fig B), continue with the inside row as follows: E, E, F, E, G, E, F, E, E, E, G, E, E, E, F, E, G, E, E, F, E, E, G, E, F, E, E, E, G, F, E, E, E (centre) G.

3. Repeat up the other side. Having placed the centre bead, needle up the 3 beads on the other side and around the centre right angle again to strengthen (Fig C).

4. When you have put in the last bead in the right angle, go around the clasp again, and make your way to the second row.

5. The pearls and the crystals must lie the same way, so it will be the reverse. The first half will be down the side, lay and down again (Fig D) as follows: E, E, E, G, F, E, E, E, F, G, E, E, E, F, E, G, E, E, F, E, E, G, E, F, E, E, E, G, F, E, (centre) G.

6. When you get to the centre, put in the focal piece and lay the centre pearl. Out of the centre angle, pick up 1F, 1G, 1J, 1H, 1C, over the C and back up H, J, G, and F, go around the right angle and back down the focal piece and up again to strengthen (Fig E). Repeat the pearls and crystals up the other side.

Optional extra

Work around the end right angle and down out of the first join.

1. Pick up 1D, go back up the right angle join (F), through the top and down the next side.

2. Pick up 1C, and back up the right angle join, through the top.

3. Repeat steps 1 and 2 (Fig F), and then down through the second row and around through the base first right angle, pick up 1 D, up the first row, pick up 1C, go through the first row, around the top down the inside row, pick up 1C and out the bottom. 1C in each space in the middle. Alternate the outside with 1D, 1C. Work away the thread.

Suzanna ear-rings

These dear little ear rings are made up of tiny right-angle cubes on a piece of fine silver, and are quick to make. Once you have made a pair, every one will be asking for them, and just by changing the little 11° seed bead you will have a very different look. You can also wear the ear ring attached to a piece of chain around the neck, brought together with a jump ring or another cube. Have fun making them!

You will need
35C 15° seed beads
18B 11° seed beads
50A 4-mm Rondell Preciosa crystals
5D 4-mm round Preciosa fire crystals
12 cm silver medium fine chain (that will allow a 6-mm jump ring through)
2 silver ear-ring studs
2x6-mm jump rings
Chain-nose pliers and cutters
Monofil thread 40
#10 Beading needle

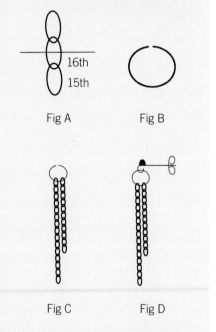

Fig A   Fig B

Fig C   Fig D

Part 1

1. Cut the chain into 2 pieces with 15 links each (cut in the 16th link – Fig A).

2. Cut another 2 pieces with 10 links each (so cut in the 11th link).

3. Open two jump rings (Fig B) and place the last link of one long piece and one short piece of chain into each opened jump ring (Fig C).

4. Place the assembled chain and jump ring into the ear-ring stud (Fig D) and close the jump rings.

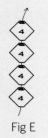

Fig E

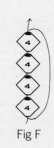

Fig F

Fig G

Fig H

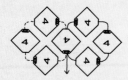

Fig J

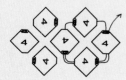

Fig K

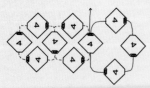

Fig L

Part 2

1. Thread up with about 1,3 m, pick up 4A and take them down your thread, leaving a tail of about 20 cm (Fig E). Take your needle back up the beads, from the tail side up (Fig F), and pull up to form a circle (Fig G).

2. Now work on around another 3 beads (Fig H); the bead you end up in will be called the leader bead (which changes with every stitch). The leader bead points in the direction in which you will be working in. The thread comes out of the bottom of the leader bead.

3. Pick up another 3A and in an anti-clockwise direction join the beads down the leader bead (Fig J) and continue on around 2 more beads to the new leader (Fig K).

4. Pick up 3A, and in a clockwise direction join up to the leader (Fig L), go on around 2 more beads (Fig M).

5. You will now join the beads to form a circle (Fig N).
a. Pick up 1A, and join up the first centre A bead, in the first right angle.
b. Pick up another 1A, work back to the old leader in step 4 and go down the centre A bead in the third right angle. You should have a cube (Fig O).
c. Work back to where the tail thread was and make a reef knot. Strengthen your cube by going around the right angles again (it will look more like a ball) ending up next to the tail thread. This is the bottom of the cube.

6. Pick up 1B and go through 1A 4 times, one in each corner (Fig P). This is the bottom done, now do the top.

7 Having put in your last B and gone through 1A, go through 1B again, pick up a fire crystal D then 3C and take the needle through the last chain link at the end of the longest chain (Fig Q).

8 Pick up 3C again, go back down the fire crystal D, and through the other side of the B bead. Repeat back up the fire crystal and the C beads, and down again, so there are two lots of thread joining the chain to the cube. Work the thread back into the body of the ear ring, knot twice, travel and cut. I dab a little nail varnish on the last pull through of the thread to stop it working out.

9 Now work another cube and attach it to the other shorter chain.

10 Make the next ear ring, but do remember to mirror the earrings. I placed the long chains on the inside.

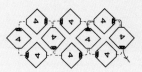

Fig M

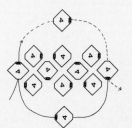

Fig N

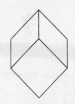

Fig O

Fig P

Fig Q

Suzette crystal necklace

This charming necklace is made up with lots of crystals, as right-angle weave lends it self so well to working with crystals. There are two balls made up with a count of six beads in the right angle, with a very simply strung strand of beads, using all different crystals. The balls are made up in two different bands, one from east to west, and the other from north to south, joined together in each cross-over north, south, east, west. These little balls would make lovely ear rings to match, using the bottom part of the necklace with a drop instead of a heart. I used beads of many different sizes in this necklace, and as you can see, just by varying the right angle as with the Suzanna ear rings, you obtain a different look. Monofil thread is used to ensure that the thread would not be visible through the crystals.

You will need

30K 15° seed beads (same as A)
150A 11° seed beads (matching second colour)
60B 4-mm crystal bicones (main colour)
15C 4-mm crystal bicones (second colour)
5D 6-mm round crystals (main colour)
6E 6-mm round beads (main colour)
2F 8-mm crystal bicones (main colour)
1J 14-mm crystal heart (main colour)
5 m Madeira monofil 40
Nymo B thread
#10 beading needle

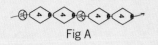

Fig A

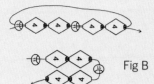

Fig B

Fig C

Fig D

Fig E

Fig F

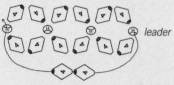

Fig G

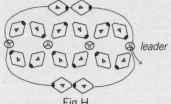

Fig H

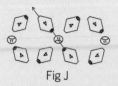

Fig J

Make the crystal balls

1. Thread up with 1,3 m monofil. Pick up 1A, 2B, 1A, 2B (6 beads) and take them down your thread leaving a tail of about 20cm (Fig A). Take the needle back up the same beads from the tail side up and pull tight so that the beads form a circle (Fig B), and then go on around 4 more beads, to the new leader bead (Fig C). You will always end in the leader – the thread comes out of the bottom of the leader bead.

2. Pick up 2B, 1A, 2B and in an anti-clockwise direction join the beads by going down through the top of the A bead, the leader (Fig D), then go on around 3 more beads 2B, and 1A, to the new leader – the thread comes out of the top of the A leader bead (Fig E).

3. Pick up 2B, 1A, 2B and in a clockwise direction join to the leader A, going up through A, and on around 3 more beads, 2B and 1A (Fig F), to the new leader A bead (3 right angles).

4. You will now join the band into a circle in two parts, first the bottom half (Fig G), and then back for the top half (Fig H). The thread comes out of the bottom of the leader.

Step 1

Step 1

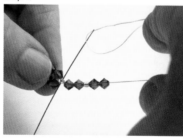

Step 2

Step 2

Step 3

Step 3

a. Pick up 2B, take the needle to join up with the first A at the start of the band and go up through the A (Fig G).

b. Pick up 2B (the top half of the join) and go back to the old leader. You've made your first band from east to west. Strengthen it by going around all the right angles again. End by going through an A and then a B in the middle of a right angle (Fig J)

5. You will make the second band from the middle of the existing band, going from north to south and connecting in the middle at the back. You have half of a right angle already made; you need 2 right angles for the top and 2 for the bottom, so you will make the other half. Your thread comes out of 1B – one half of the right angle (Fig M). Pick up 1B, 1A, 1B and join down the other half of the right angle (Fif N), down through 1B, and then on around through 2B and 1A, back to the new leader (Fig M). This is the first half of the lid. Now the other right angle to close into the back.

6. Make the other half. Turn your work so that the worked piece is at the back, and you have an empty front. Your thread still comes out of A (Fig N). Pick up 1B and go through the attached B on the same side as the thread in the front,

Fig L

Fig M

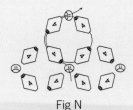

Fig N

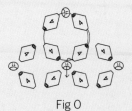

Fig O

Step 3b

Step 4a

Step 4b

Step 4b end

Step 5a

Step 5a top bead

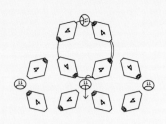

Fig O

then up the next attached B on the band (the other half of the right angle). Pick up another B and join to A (the old leader) which is now the centre of the lid.

7. Work your way to the top of the E-W band and continue with the N-S band. Make the bottom lid. Your thread comes out of a B in the N-S band (Fig P). Repeat steps 5 and 6.

8. Strengthen by going around all the right angles again. Your little ball should be reasonably firm. Knot the thread twice and work away. Make another ball.

Step b

Step 7 a

Step 7b second half

Step 7 on around

Step 7 back to top

One side of top

Up next side

Fasten last one in

Completed

Assemble the piece

I prefer using Nymo thread to assemble the piece as the hangings always look a bit stiff if worked with monfil. Thread up with Nymo and work the thread in, coming out of an A bead on the ball to attch the balls together.

1. Pick up 1C, 2A, 1D, 2A, 1C, go through the A bead in the second ball and back up 1C, 2A, 1D, 2A, and1C, then make your way out of the A bead on the other side of the first ball to make the hanging tail (Fig P).

2. Pick up 1C, 1A, 4K, go through the heart, pick up another 4K, go through the A bead, up the C, and through the A attached to the ball (Fig Q). Repeat the thread path to strengthen, go up the ball and through the joining beads to the next ball and end off in the ball. Knot

3. To prepare the clasp for the string of beads, thread up with 3 m Nymo (it must all be done on one piece of thread, so take care and pull slowly to avoid knots). Put on a stop bead, going through the bead twice (with the eye of the needle to avoid splitting the thread). Pick up 1E, 1B, 1C, 10A, 1B, 4K, the clasp, and 4K again (Fig R). Now go back towards the stop bead, needle through the B, 10A, 1C, 1B, 1E and make a half hitch (Fig S). Do not go through the stop bead. Leave to the side.

4. For the string of beads:
a. Pick up1B, 1C, 10A, 1B, 1A, 1D, 1A, 1B
b. Pick up 8A, 1C, 1B, 1E, 1B, 1C
c. Pick up 8A, 1B, 1A, 1D, 1A, 1B
d. Pick up 8A, 1C, 1B, 1E, 1B, 1C
e. Pick up 8A, 1B, 1A, 1F, 1A, 1B, 6A, and through the centre A on the ball.
f. Repeat steps 4e, d, c, b and a on the other side of the string of beads to match the first side, reading them back to front (for example 4e is 6A, 1B, 1A, 1F, 1A, 1B, 8A.

5. Prepare the other side of the clasp. Pick up 1E, 1B, 1C, 10A, 1B, 4K, the clasp, another 4K, go back through the 1B, 10A, 1C, 1B and make a half hitch (Fig S).

6. Now take the thread down all the beads to the centre (do not go through the centre bead), pick up 1A, and up the other side, to the top. Tie to the tail thread, having removed the stop bead. Go through the clasp and all the way through the entire necklace again, including the centre bead (if the thread or needle will allow you to), otherwise use the top bead, up to the other side, through the clasp again, and make a few half hitches in the first set of big beads. Put a little dab of nail varnish on the last pull through.

7. Tidy the tail piece in the same way.

Fig P

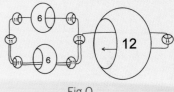

Fig Q

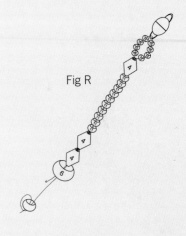

Fig R

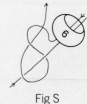

Fig S

Petrusa evening bag

This attractive little bag is made up with four-count right-angle weave, and gives you good practice with the stitch. It looks very effective if you play with colour. If you wish, you could sew a lining, turn it inside out and attach it to the beads on the inside. I made the entire bag in Gutermann 9° seed beads, and embellished it with a single row of stone chips. You start working at the top.

You will need

2650A 9° Gutermann seed beads (main colour)
400B 9° Gutermann seed beads (first colour)
300C 9° Gutermann seed beads (second colour)
300D 9° Gutermann seed beads (third colour)
900E 9° Gutermann seed beads (fourth colour)
75 stone chips
2 round 6-mm beads for ends
Nymo B thread
Cord for draw string
#10 or 11 needle

Fig A   **Fig B**

Fig C

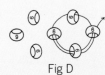

Fig D

Row 1

1. Pick up 4A, leaving a tail of 20 cm, and pass the needle up the same 4 again, from the tail end up (Fig A). Bring the beads into a circle, and continue around another 3 beads (1 right angle – Fig B). The bead farthest to the right will be called the leader bead (which is the bead your thread is out of).

2. Pick up 3A (as one bead is already there) and continue the circle round and through the old leader (joining bead – Fig C and on around through the next 2 beads (Fig D). This will bring the thread to the foreground to the new leader.

3. Make 63 right angles altogether, all in A. (See page 110 Figs A-H as each right agle is different, one clockwise, the other anti-clockwise.)

4. The last right angle will join the two ends to make a tube. Take care not to twist it. Pick up 1A and join to the other end (Fig E). Pick up another A bead, join to the first end (Fig F) and take your needle to the left (Fig G). Tie to the tail.

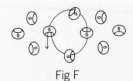

Fig E

Row 2

1. Turn your work so that your thread comes out at the bottom, pick up 3A only (as 1 bead is there already) and join to the top bead (Fig H). Go on around one more bead. This will be the new leader (Fig Ji and ii).

2. From now on you will pick up only 2 beads each time (as 2 are there already). Pick up 2A and join to the bottom of the previous row (Fig K), and then to the old leader (4 beads - right angle), and on around 2 more beads ((Fig L). This will be your new leader.

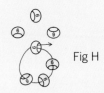

Fig F

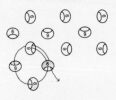

Fig G

Fig H

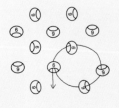

Fig K

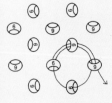

Fig L

Fig Ji   **Fig Jii**

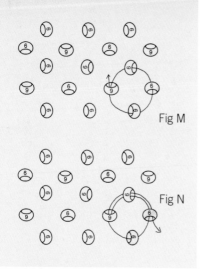

Fig M

Fig N

3. Next the circle will go the other way. Join to the bottom of the previous row, then pick up 2A and join to the old leader (4 beads – Fig M), take your needle on around another 2 beads to the new leader (Fig N).

4. Repeat steps 2 and 3 all in A until you have 63 right angles.

5. To join the two sides there will be 3 beads already there (Fig O) from your old leader. Pick up 1A and join to the other side (the first bead of the row) then go through the top bead of the previous row and lastly back to the old leader (Fig P) and on around 1 more bead. You now have 64 right angles.

Row 1, step 1

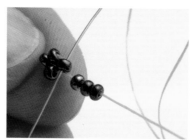

Step 2, add next right angle

And on around

Step 3

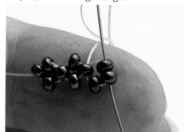

On around

Step 4, close the two sides, bottom half

Step 4, top half

Step 4, on around

Row 2, step 1

And on around one more

Row 2, step 2

And on around

Row 3

Repeat row 2 all in A. Make sure you have 64 right angles.

Starting a new thread

If your thread is getting short, come out of the new leader bead, and make a little knot (a half hitch of a French knot) and leave. Take a new thread of about 2,5 m and go back three right angles. Go through two beads in the right angle and knot (Fig Qi), up the next 3 beads in the next right angle and knot again, and up the last 2 beads, continue (Fig Qii). Then go back and finish the old thread in the same way, only take it into the new work.

Row 4

(using A and B seed beads)

1. From the bead at the bottom of the previous row, pick up 3A, go round and join to the bead you started on (4 beads – Fig Ri) and on round 1 more bead, to the new leader (Fig Rii).

2. Pick up 2B, join to the top from right to left, go on round to the old leader A (4 beads – Fig Si), and on around two more coming out of the B bead (the new leader – Fig Sii).

3. Join to the top A, pick up 2A, join to the old leader B (4 beads – Fig Ti) and go on around 2 more beads, ending in the new leader (Fig Tii)

4. Repeat steps 2 and 3 in B and A beads 13 times, which results in 29 right angles. Finish on A.

5. Repeat 2 and 3 twice, using only A beads = 33 right angles.

6. Repeat 2 and 3 in B and A beads 14 times = 61 right angles.

7. Repeat steps 2 and 3 all in A once = 63 right angles

8. To join, pick up 1A and join to the other side, go through the bottom bead in the previous row, and back to the old leader (4 beads – Fig Ui), and on around 1 more bead (Fig Uii). You are now ready for the next row with 64 right angles as in row 2, step 5. You should have 14B stripes front and back and 5 right angles in A for the spine.

Row 5

(note how with each start of the row you move over by 1)

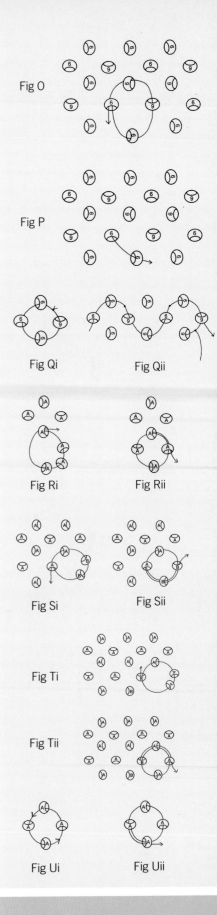

Fig O

Fig P

Fig Qi   Fig Qii

Fig Ri   Fig Rii

Fig Si   Fig Sii

Fig Ti

Fig Tii

Fig Ui   Fig Uii

ROW	STEPS	BEAD COLOURS	REPETITIONS	RESULT
5	Repeat row 4, steps 1 and 2	A only	1	2 right angles
	Repeat row 4 steps 3 and 2	B for step 3, A for step 2	14	30 right angles
	Repeat row 4 steps 3 and 2	A only	2	34 right angles
	Repeat row 4 steps 3 and 2	B for step 3, A for step 2	14	62 right angles
	Repeat row 4 step 3	A only	1	63 right angles
	Join as in Row 4 step 3	A only		64 right angles
6	Repeat row 4, steps 1, 2 and 3	A only	1	3 right angles
	Repeat row 4 steps 2 and 3	B and A	14	31 right angles
	Repeat row 4 steps 2 and 3	A only	2	35 right angles
	Repeat row 4 steps 2 and 3	B and A	14	63 right angles
	Join as in row 4 step 8	A only		64 right angles
7 Change colour, C instead of B	Repeat row 4, steps 1, 2 and 3	A only	1 + step 2 again	3 right angles
	Repeat row 4 steps 3 and 2	C for step 3, A for step 2	14	32 right angles
	Repeat row 4 steps 3 and 2	A only	2	36 right angles
	Repeat row 4 steps 3 and 2	C for step 3, A for step 2	13 + step 3 again	63 right angles
	Join as in row 4 step 3	A only		64 right angles
8 Start in just stripes	Repeat row 4, step 1	Pick up 2A and 1C	1	1 right angle
	Repeat row 4 steps 2 and 3	A only	2	5 right angles
	Repeat row 4 steps 2 and 3	C for step 2, A for step 3	14	33 right angles
	Repeat row 4 steps 2 and 3	A only	2	37 right angles
	Repeat row 4 steps 2 and 3	C for step 2, A for step 3	13	63 right angles
	Join as in row 4 step 8	Pick up 1C		64 right angles
9 Change colour, D instead of C	Start in just stripes			
	Repeat row 4, step 1	Pick up 2D and 1A	1	1 right angle
	Repeat row 4 steps 2 and 3	A only	2	5 right angles
	Repeat row 4 step 2	A only	1	6 right angles
	Repeat row 4 steps 3 and 2	D for step 3, A for step 2	14	34 right angles
	Repeat row 4 steps 3 and 2	A only	2	38 right angles
	Repeat row 4 steps 3 and 2	D for step 3, A for step 2	12	62 right angles
	Repeat row 4 step 3	D	1	63 right angles
	Join as in row 4 step 8	A		64 right angles
10 Start in A stripe (2nd in)	Repeat row 4, step 1	Pick up 2A and 1D	1	1 right angle
	Repeat row 4 step 2	D only	1	2 right angles
	Repeat row 4 steps 3 and 2	A only	2	6 right angles
	Repeat row 4 step 3	A only	1	7 right angles
	Repeat row 4 steps 2 and 3	D and A	14	35 right angles
	Repeat row 4 steps 2 and 3	A only	2	39 right angles

ROW	STEPS	BEAD COLOURS	REPETITIONS	RESULT
	Repeat row 4 steps 2 and 3	D and A	12	63 right angles
	Join as in row 4 step 8	D		64 right angles
11 Start in D stripe (3rd in)	Repeat row 4, step 1	Pick up 2D and 1A	1	1 right angle
	Repeat row 4 steps 2 and 3	A for step 2, D for step 3	1	3 right angles
	Repeat row 4 steps 2 and 3	A only	2	7 right angles
	Repeat row 4 step 2	A only	1	8 right angles
	Repeat row 4 steps 3 and 2	D for step 3, A for step 2	14	36 right angles
	Repeat row 4 steps 3 and 2	A only	2	40 right angles
	Repeat row 4 steps 3 and 2	D for step 3, A for step 2	11	62 right angles
	Repeat row 4 step 3	A only	1	63 right angles
	Join as in row 4 step 8	A		64 right angles
12 Change colour, E instead of D	Repeat row 4, step 1	Pick up 2A and 1E	1	1 right angle
	Repeat row 4 steps 2 and 3	E for step 2, A for step 3	1	3 right angles
	Repeat row 4 step 2	Net E	1	4 right angles
	Repeat row 4 steps 3 and 2	A only	2	8 right angles
	Repeat row 4 step 3	A only	1	9 right angles
	Repeat row 4 steps 2 and 3	E for step 2, A for step 3	14	37 right angles
	Repeat row 4 steps 2 and 3	A only	2	41 right angles
	Repeat row 4 steps 2 and 3	E for step 2, A for step 3	11	63 right angles
	Join as in row 4 step 8	E		64 right angles
13 Start in E stripe (5th in)	Repeat row 4, step 1	Pick up 2E and 1A	1	1 right angle
	Repeat row 4 steps 2 and 3	A for step 2, E for step 3	2	5 right angles
	Repeat row 4 steps 2 and 3	A only	2	9 right angles
	Repeat row 4 step 2	A only	1	10 right angles
	Repeat row 4 steps 3 and 2	E for step 3, A for step 2	14	38 right angles
	Repeat row 4 steps 3 and 2	A only	2	42 right angles
	Repeat row 4 steps 3 and 2	E for step 3, A for step 2	10	62 right angles
	Repeat row 4 step 3	Net E	1	63 right angles
	Join as in row 4 step 8	A		64 right angles
14 Start in A stripe (6th in)	Repeat row 4, step 1	Pick up 2A and 1E	1	1 right angle
	Repeat row 4 steps 2 and 3	E for step 2, A for step 3	2	5 right angles
	Repeat row 4 step 2	Net E		6 right angles
	Repeat row 4 steps 3 and 2	A only	2	10 right angles
	Repeat row 4 step 3	A only	1	11 right angles
	Repeat row 4 steps 2 and 3	E for step 2, A for step 3	14	39 right angles
	Repeat row 4 steps 2 and 3	A only	2	43 right angles
	Repeat row 4 steps 2 and 3	E for step 2, A for step 3	10	63 right angles

ROW	STEPS	BEAD COLOURS	REPETITIONS	RESULT
	Join as in row 4 step 8	E		64 right angles
15 Start in E stripe (7th in)	Repeat row 4, step 1	Pick up 2E and 1A	1	1 right angle
	Repeat row 4 steps 2 and 3	A for step 2, E for step 3	3	7 right angles
	Repeat row 4 steps 2 and 3	A only	2	11 right angles
	Repeat row 4 step 2	A only	1	12 right angles
	Repeat row 4 steps 3 and 2	E for step 3, A for step 2	14	40 right angles
	Repeat row 4 steps 3 and 2	A only	2	44 right angles
	Repeat row 4 steps 3 and 2	E for step 3, A for step 2	9	62 right angles
	Repeat row 4 step 3	Net E	1	63 right angles
	Join as in row 4 step 8	A		64 right angles

In row 16 you will change colour again and also move the stripe over by 1, which means you will reduce the spine by 1 right angle and there will be an extra stripe on the back and front. You will go back to using colours A, and B.

ROW	STEPS	BEAD COLOURS	REPETITIONS	RESULT
16	Repeat row 4, step 1	2B and 1A (this will fall under the A stripe)	1	1 right angle
	Repeat row 4 steps 2 and 3	A for step 2, B for step 3	4	9 right angles
	Repeat row 4 steps 2 and 3	A only	1	11 right angles
	Repeat row 4 step 2	A only	1	12 right angles
	Repeat row 4 steps 3 and 2	B for step 3, A for step 2	14	40 right angles
	Repeat row 4 step 3	B only (note when attaching the top bead the colour has changed	1	41 right angles
	Repeat row 4 steps 2 and 3	A only	1	43 right angles
	Repeat row 4 step 2	A only	1	44 right angles
	Repeat row 4 steps 3 and 2	B for step 3, A for step 2	9	62 right angles
	Repeat row 4 step 3	B only	1	63 right angles
	Join as in row 4 step 8	A		64 right angles

Row 17

Continue in this manner. Pick up 2A and 1B, and make 64 right angles in the same colour sequence as row 16, namely 15 stripes in A and B plus 3 in A for the spine, and joining in B.

Row 18

Pick up 2B and 1A, and continue with picking up 2A and then 2B, keeping the pattern going with 15 stripes and the spine consisting of 3 right angles. Join in A at the end of the row.

Fig A

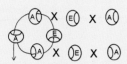

Fig B

Fig C

Fig D

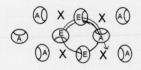

Fig E

Fig F

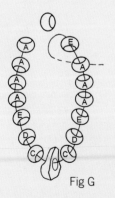

Fig G

Row 19

Change colour, using A and C. Pick up 2A and 1C, continue with picking up 2C and then 2A, following the pattern of stripe and spine 3 right angles for the rest of the bag. Join in C at the end of the row.

Row 20

Pick up 2C and 1A, follow the pattern and continue with picking up 2A and then 2C, not forgetting the spine. Join in A at the end of the row.

Row 21

Change colour. Pick up 2A and 1D, follow the pattern and continue with picking up 2D and then 2A. Join in D. Check the spine.

Row 22

Pick up 2D and 1A, follow the pattern and continue with 2A then 2D. Join in A.

Row 23

Pick up 2A and 1D, follow the pattern and continue, joining in D.

Row 24

Change colour. Pick up 2E and 1A, follow the pattern and continue, joining in A.

Row 25

Pick up 2A and 1E, follow the pattern and continue, joining in E

Row 26

Pick up 2E and 1A, follow the pattern and continue, joining in A.

Row 27

Pick up 2A and 1E, follow the pattern and continue, joining in E.

Some beads are a little smaller than others, so the two last rows are optional.

Row 28

Pick up 2E and 1A, follow the pattern and continue, joining in A.

Row 29

Pick up 2A and 1E, follow the pattern and continue, joining in E.

Joining the sides

1. With the weaving complete, you can now join the bottom ends. Weave your thread into the middle bead in the spine, A bead, and fold in half. You will join all the beads to one another, closing the end. Having the thread come out of the A bead at the end, you will make right angles to close the bag. Fig A shows what you have and you need to put a bead in the middle of all the x's.

2. Make a right angle: go through an A bead, pick up an E bead and go back through an A bead and back to the old leader (A bead – Fig B) your thread came out of, and go on around two more beads to the new leader E bead (Fig C).

3. Now the other way. Go through an E bead, pick up an A and back up through the E, and into the old leader E (Fig D), on around two more beads to the new leade (A bead) (Fig E).

4. Continue in this way until you have closed the bag.

Add embellishments and finish

1. To make the tassels at the bottom, I used a loop. Take a new thread and weave into the end bead again, into an A bead (Fig F). Pick up 3A,(1C, 1D, 1E,) the combination in brackets can be changed, plus 1 chip, then reverse the combination, (1E, 1D, 1C), 3A and fasten it to the next right angle E bead (Fig G), taking the thread through the bead away from you. Bring the needle through the loop you have just made towards you , and repeat the process ending on the last A bead(Fig H).

2. Add the embellishments along the middle of the bag. Weave the needle to the B bead. Having gone through, facing up, on the right hand side, pick up 1E, 1 chip, 1E, and go down through the opposite A bead in the same right angle. Weave from that leader to the next leader, (E bead), and repeat (Fig J).

3. Embellish the top. Out of the two middle right angles in the back (Fig K), work ten rows of right angles, and then secure the chips to the ends, making the middle one the longest one out of the end of the two right angles, and the last out of the middle bead. This will feed through the loops in front to close.

4. Make the loops around the top of the bag, making sure that the bead on the end of your cord fits through, or work over the cord.

Fig H

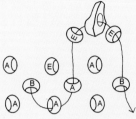

Fig J

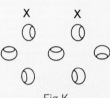

Fig K

Diana watch

This pretty little watch is made up mainly with right-angle weave that has been divided. It is important that the right angle is made with an odd number for the strap to come together nicely. The strap is made up with nothing bigger than a 4-mm bead, and hence is quite soft. The centre is filled with different beads. Without a watch face this would also make a lovely bracelet. You can also make it longer for a choker – then hang a crystal pear drop or heart off the centre. When measuring the length of a watch strap or choker, I find it useful to take a piece of string, measure it for a comfortable length, and use this as a guide.

You will need
295A 11° seed beads
70B 11° seed beads
70C 15° seed beads
25D 4-mm round crystals
25E Baby Drops
Watch face
Clasp
Nymo beading thread
#11 needle 11

Make the strap

1. Thread up with a nice long thread of about 2 m. Pick up 4A and take them down the thread, leaving a tail of about 30 cm (Fig Ai). Go back up the same 4 beads, from the tail side up (Fig Aii), bring the beads into a circle (Fig Aiii), and continue on around another 3 beads (1 right angle). The bead that your thread ends up in will be called the leader (Fig Aiv). The leader will always point in the direction in which you are to work.

2. Pick up another 3A beads (the thread comes out of the bottom of the leader), make a circle in an anti-clockwise direction and take the needle down the leader (Fig Bi), pull up and continue in an anti-clockwise direction through 2 more beads (Fig Bii). This will bring the thread to the foreground to the new leader (2 right angles).

3. Pick up 3A (as one bead is already there), the thread comes out of the top of the leader, make a circle in a clockwise direction and take the needle up the leader (Fig Ci). Pull up and continue in a clockwise direction through 2 more beads (Fig Cii). This will bring the thread to the foreground and to the new leader.

4. Note how one circle is made in an anti-clockwise direction, and the next in a clockwise direction. Continue with steps 2 and 3 until the strap is long enough for your arm, not forgetting the clasp. I have small wrists, and I made mine 15 right angles.

5. Pick up another 3A, and take them round and join to the leader (Fig Di), and then on around 3 more beads (the bead next to the old leader – you are changing direction – Fig Dii). That is side one.

6. Start side two. Make another right angle, pick up 3A and take them round and join to the leader (Fig Ei), and on around 1 more A (Fig Eii). You are changing direction again and you should have 2 right angles side by side sharing a common bead. You will now work back towards the beginning making the second side.

7. Pick up 3A and take them on around and join to the leader (Fig Fi), and then on around 2 more beads (Fig Fii). (I prefer to turn my work so that I am working from left to right.) Make another 13 right angles (14 right angles so far).

8. Pick up another 3A to make the last right angle, and join to the leader (Fig Gi), and on around 1 more bead (Fig Gii). This will bring you to the bead on the inside, nearest side 1.

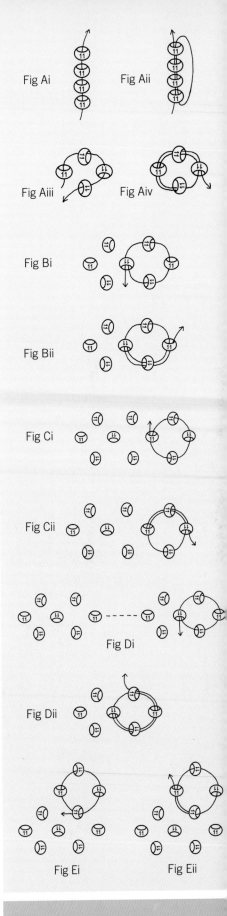

Fig Ai   Fig Aii

Fig Aiii   Fig Aiv

Fig Bi

Fig Bii

Fig Ci

Fig Cii

Fig Di

Fig Dii

Fig Ei   Fig Eii

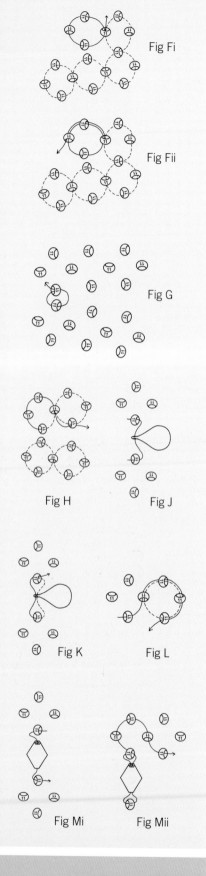

Fig Fi

Fig Fii

Fig G

Fig H

Fig J

Fig K

Fig L

Fig Mi

Fig Mii

9. You will now join the two beads with a ladder stitch, down side 1, up side 2 (Fig G). Turn your work again so that you are working left to right, and go around 3 more beads, plus 1 into the next right angle (Fig H). This is the bead where you will start to fill the centre, and each bead has an opposite on the other side.

10. Pick up 1E drop, go through the opposite bead on the same side as the thread (Fig J), and back through the drop, and into the first bead on the other side (Fig K). Then go on around 4 more beads to the new right angle, to the bead facing the opening (Fig L).

11. Pick up 1D crystal, go through the opposite bead on the same side as the thread (Fig Mi), and back through the crystal D, and into the bead on the first side (Fig Mii). Then go on around 4 more beads to the new right angle, to the bead facing the opening.

12. Repeat steps 10 and 11 until you have filled up the opening, ending on a drop. Having put in the last drop, continue on around to the end bead of the right angle. This is where you will attach the watch face (Fig N).

13. Pick up 1A, and go through the watch face plus 1A, and through the same bead on the other side in the right angle (Fig O).

14. Go back through the picked up bead, through the watch and through the second picked up bead on the other side, and into the right angle on the other side of the thread, then on around (Fig P).

15. Repeat step 13: go through the picked up bead and watch and picked up bead and through the first bead in the right angle, and around the right angle (Fig Q), then make your way to the outer bead on the outer edge of the right angle (Fig R).

16. Pick up a crystal D and attach to the same bead on the other side (it should lay across 1 bead), needle through the bead, needle facing towards the watch (Fig S).

17. Pick up a crystal D, take the needle through the watch, pick up another crystal D and attach to the right angle bead from which you started in step 16 (Fig T).

18. Repeat the circle around the watch 2 more times to strengthen, ending up in the first bead in step 16 (Fig U).

Fig N

Fig O

Fig P

Fig Q

Fig R

Fig S

Fig T

Fig U

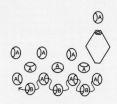

Fig A

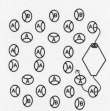

Fig B

Fig C

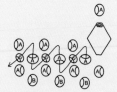

Fig D

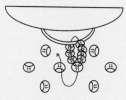

Fig E

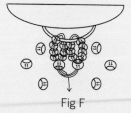

Fig F

Add embellishments

1. Pick up 1B and go through 1A on the outer edge. If you made 15 right angles, then insert 14B. Go down one side, and up the other (Fig A), taking care not to pull too tight, but keeping the tension.

2. Having picked up the 14th B, take the needle through the bottom A bead at the bed of the crystal, up through the crystal and out the same bead on the other side, and through the next bead of the right angle of the crystal bed, needle facing in to the centre (Fig B).

3. Embellish the top. Pick up 1C and lay it diagonally across the right angle, and needle through the next right angle bead, lying in the same direction (Fig C).

4. Put in 14C beads, the same number as B, which should firm up the strap (Fig D).

Attach the clasp

1. At the end where you laddered the 2 right angles together, thread (tail end) out of the one bead, and pick up 6 or 7C (depending on the size of the clasp) plus the clasp end, and go back through the same bead (Fig E).

2. Take the needle up the next bead beside it (one of the two laddered beads) and repeat. Pick up 6 or 7C and through the clasp and back through the same bead (Fig F).

3. Repeat steps 1 and 2 so that you have at least 2 threads running through each loop over the clasp.

Repeat all the steps to make the other half of the strap.